An Index

to the

Complete Works

of

al-Imām al-Mahdi

Fergus Nicoll

Nusairi Publishing
London

First published in Great Britain in 2009 by

Nusairi Publishing
21 Grosvenor Crescent
Kingsbury
London NW9 9DB

All rights reserved

No part of this publication may be reproduced, stored or transmitted in any for, without the express written permission of the publisher.

Copyright © Fergus Nicoll

The moral right of Fergus Nicoll to be recognised as the author of this work has been asserted in accordance with the Copyright, Design and Patents Act, 1988.

ISBN: 1-871-074-25-8

Typeset in Gentium

Contents

Introduction	i
Volume 1	1
Volume 2	27
Volume 3	46
Volume 4	68
Volume 5	109
Volume 6	148
Volume 7	153
Index to Names	156
Index to Topics	173

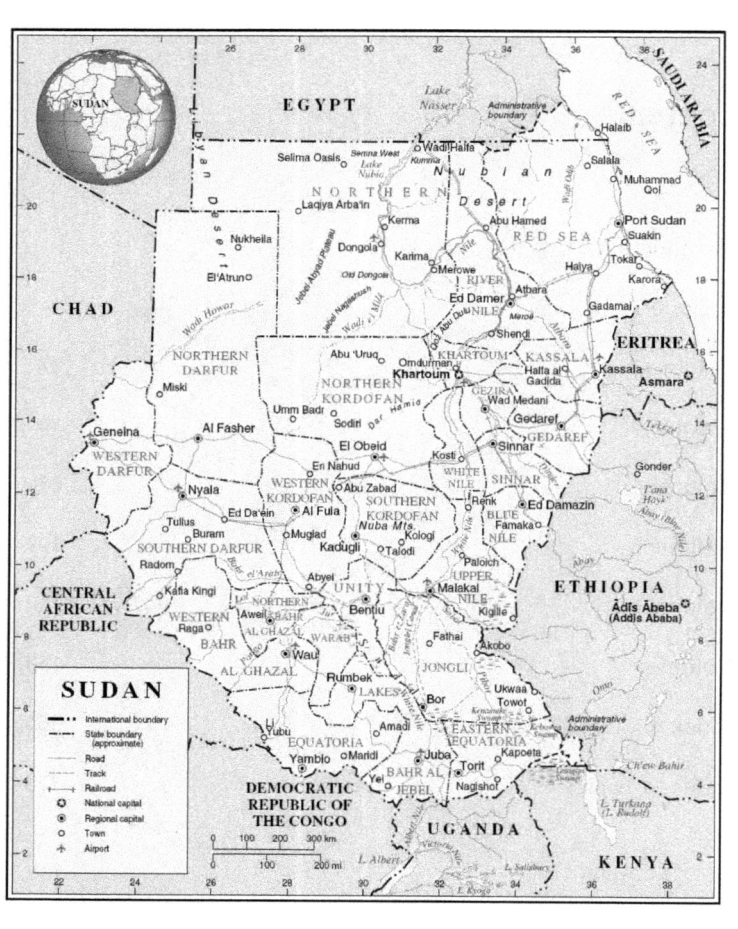

Introduction

The following pages present the first English-language index to Professor Muhammad Ibrāhīm Abū-Salīm's seven-volume anthology, *Al-Athār al-Kāmila li'l-Imām al-Mahdi* ("The Collected Works of the Imām al-Mahdi", Khartoum, KUP, 1990-94). While many of the letters and edicts contained had been previously published in editions dating back to the bound "letter-books" carried by senior loyalists during the Mahdīa itself, Professor Abū-Salīm's magisterial research and presentation, organised largely in chronological order, can claim to be the definitive collection and commentary.

The material spans a period from 1875 – when Muhammad Ahmad ibn ʿAbdallah was a 31-year-old sheikh and community leader based at Jazīra Aba on the White Nile – to his death at Omdurman on 22 June 1885 (9 Ramadan 1302), by which time he had ejected Sudan's colonial occupiers and instated his own, unique brand of Islamic rule. The Mahdi's writings can be broadly divided into proclamations designed for mass consumption and often circulated in large numbers (manshūrāt) and private letters (risāʾil). These may further be subdivided and classed under a variety of headings including warnings (indharāt), legal rulings (ahkām) and visions (hadhrāt).

The Mahdi's writings, anthologised in Volumes 1 to 5, cover a vast range of political, spiritual, economic, social and administrative territory. It is quite clear from both range and depth that he remained until the last the decisive and controlling voice within the movement on all aspects of life. Thus, in a typical period between March and April 1885 (Volume 4), he writes on the collection of badly-needed grain in Kordofan, the deployment of forces to Dongola, the annulment of a marriage, judicial rulings on land disputes and pardoning the family of the veteran slaver al-Zubeir Rahmatallah Mansūr, while still taking time to offer personal condolences to bereaved followers. The recipients of these outpourings include all the Mahdīa's leading military, religious and administrative personalities, as well as a broad cross-section of tribal leaders both hostile and friendly.

The sheer scale of output indicates the crucial importance of the written word, mass-produced on the printing presses of the occupying Turkīa, in conveying authoritative communications across large distances in nineteenth-century Africa. It also suggests the involvement of an impressively organised central secretariat in which individual scribes were permitted a certain latitude in the phrasing and tone of individual messages, an impression confirmed by the variety of hands, verbal styles and degrees of literary sophistication evident in the letters and edicts.

Volumes 6 and 7 present rather different material. First to be set out in full is the Rātib, a concise volume of mandatory prayers, incantations and quotations from the Qur'ān that was intended precisely to serve as a communal binding agent. After the Rātib and associated supplications come 41 sermons (khutab), which fill out the Mahdi's message on important issues such as jihād, the centrality of the Sunna and the worthless nature of the material world.

Volume 7 continues this theme – contrasting with the written record of the manshūrāt, letters and Rātib – of the Mahdi's oral legacy, loosely grouped here under the heading of "sittings" (majālis). While the term implies a formal session or council (such as a parliamentary gathering today), it is used here to embrace study seminars, wise sayings, poetry and stories about the lives of the Prophet Muhammad and other holy men. The material gathered here represents but a small fraction of the Mahdi's oral teachings over the years, the bulk of it from his later life.

Dr Abū-Salīm notes that the majālis were recorded "in the period of anxiety that followed the Mahdi's death", even as letter-books and compilations of the manshūrāt began to be collated. The oral material took longer to gather, however, despite the co-operation of the Khalīfa's scribes, and did not appear until AH 1306, two years after the first publication of the written literature. The sources of this oral history are regarded as being beyond reproach; there was little to gain by putting words into the Mahdi's mouth, while there were too many contemporaries still living to risk public contradiction. Dr Abū-Salīm notes that there is nothing recorded in the majālis that is "foreign to the Mahdi's thinking".

It remains a source of fascination (and relief to researchers) that so many thousands of documents were retained with pride at a time and in a culture where a natural instinct to archiving was generally limited to the family Qur'ān and family tree. Certainly the survival of "first edition" and early copies of the Mahdi's own writings far outstrips the entire documentary database of the preceding sixty years of the Turkīa.

Finally, compilation of this Index would not have been possible without the translation skills of Osman al-Nusairi, who has been a valued collaborator on many projects over many years.

Fergus Nicoll
Oxford, 2009

Volume 1

Vol 1		173 letters (1875 - 31st October 1883)
Page	No.	Recipient – Subject matter – Dates
1	-	Preface by Mudatthir ʿAbd-al-Rahīm
5	-	Introduction to the collection by Dr Muhammad Ibrāhīm Abū-Salīm
47	1	[No recipient identified] Appointing Sirāj al-Dīn a sheikh of the Sammānīa order [During 1292] - 1875
53	2	[No recipient identified] Witnessing a document of debt settlement by sale of slave-girl 3rd Shaʿbān 1294 - 10th August 1877
54	3	[No recipient identified] A poem in appeasement of al-Sheikh Muhammad Sharīf Nūr al-Dāʿim [During 1295] - 1878-9
56	4	[No recipient identified] Power of attorney for a marriage ceremony Before the Mahdīa - before 1881
57	5	To whom it may concern Letter of protection for Batta family, in capacity as "Wali of Allah" [No date]
58	6	al-Daw ibn Suleimān, Qādi of Fashoda Asking Qādi to exempt ʿAbd-al-Nabi from government service Between 1295 and 1298 - 1878-81

Volume 1

Page	No.	Recipient – Subject matter – Dates
61	7	Ahmad ibn Muhammad al-Hāj Sharīf Ashraf relative in need of assistance from community Before Shaʻbān 1298 – before 30th June 1881

1297 – 1880

Page	No.	Recipient – Subject matter – Dates
63	8	al-Hāja Amna, daughter of al-faqi Muhammad Nūr, etc. Summons to mobilise during Ramadan 12th Rajab – 21st June
65	9	al-Sheikh Suleimān Summons to mobilise during Shawwāl at rendez-vous 14th Rajab – 22nd June
67	10	Ibrāhīm Mahmūd, Muhammad his brother and others Urgent call to heed daʻwa and mobilise 4th Dhū al-Qaʻda – 9th October
68	11	ʻAbd-al-Fatāh, son of al-faqi ʻAbdallah Deterioration of religion and reference to secrets yet to be revealed 3rd or 27th Dhū al-Qaʻda – 31st Sept or 7th Oct
71	12	Muhammad al-Tayyib al-Basīr Reference to secrets yet to be revealed and boasting huge army of spirits Dhū al-Qaʻda – 5th Oct or 4th Nov
73	13	al-Sheikh Suleimān Summons to mobilise at Jazīra Aba or al-Dueim during Muharram 13th Dhū al-Hijja – 16th November

Volume 1

Page	No.	Recipient – Subject matter - Dates
		1298 - 1881
75	14	Mūsa Muhammad al-Ahmar Consolation over house fire; sends material to replace Sufi banners Before Shaʿbān - before 30th June
76	15	Muhammad al-Tayyib al-Basīr Description of prophetic vision and summons to make hijra 1st Shaʿbān - 30th June
82	16	All the populace and those who love God [Summary of Letter 15] After 1st Shaʿbān - after 29th June
84	17	All the brethren among those who love God and religious leaders Aspects of the Mahdīa and significance of the hijra Shaʿbān - 30th June-28th July
86	18	Respected beloved in God and brethren in God's faith Refers to earlier letter about daʿwa; importance of hijra during Ramadan Shaʿbān - 30th June-28th July
88	19	Reasonable and honourable men Pursuit of pure religion; seduction of ʿulamāʾ by worldly glamour Shaʿbān - 30th June-28th July

Volume 1

Page	No.	Recipient – Subject matter - Dates
		1298 - 1881
91	20	All beloved in God and believers in God Pursuit of after-life; importance of hijra; details of his family tree Shaʿbān - 30th June-28th July
94	21	The Government [al-Hikimdārīa] Reply, mentioning proofs of Mahdism and necessity of jihād Before 10th Ramadan - before 7th August
96	22	Dafaʾallah Biqwi Signs of Mahdism and importance of mobilisation Shawwāl - 28th Aug-25th Sept
101	23	al-Sheikh Suleimān Call to mobilise and bring Fallāta [West Africans] to Jebel Tagali Before Dhū al-Hijja - before 26th October
		1299
102	24	All the [people of the] Funj Mountains Call to jihād under local leader, ʿAttā al-Manān al-Suleihābi 7th Muharram - 29th November
105	25	al-Khalīfa al-Sheikh ʿAttā al-Manān, etc. Granting authority as deputy to accept pledges of allegiance 7th Muharram - 29th November

Volume 1

Page	No.	Recipient – Subject matter - Dates
		1299 - 1882
111	26	Ahmad al-Hāj al-Badri and others Reminder of pledge and call to migrate to Jebel Gadīr 8th Rabīʿ I - 27th January
113	27	All the people of the Kalogi Hills Appointment of ʿAdam ʿAli Abū-Jakka as local deputy 12th Rabīʿ I - 1st February
115	28	People of al-Aghībish, Kalogi and Lūqāt Appointment of ʿAdam ʿAli Abū-Jakka; call to pay zakāt 21st Rabīʿ I - 10th February
117	29	ʿAsākir Abū-Kalām Rebuke for delay in hijra and for supporting the Turks 1st Jumāda I - 21st March
119	30	People of Khor al-Tayyir and Gheirhum [southern White Nile] Reminder that only infidels support the Turks; license to fight them Jumāda II - 20th March-19th May
121	31	Yūsuf Hassan al-Shallāli Point-by-point rebuttal of anti-Mahdi arguments 4th Rajab - 22nd May
129	32	Sālih walad Fadlallah, etc. [Kababish tribal leaders] Urge not to fight Juheina tribe and to return loot 20th Rajab - 8th June

Volume 1

Page	No.	Recipient – Subject matter - Dates
		1299 - 1882
130	33	Sons of Abū-al-Keilik and others [in Blue Nile region] Obey ʿAttā al-Manān and pay him zakāt 28th Rajab - 15th June
131	34	ʿAsākir Abū-Kalām Further rebuke; call to give safe passage to ʿOsmān Abū-Girja on hijra 8th Shaʿbān - 25th June
133	35	ʿAsākir Abū-Kalām Made deputy; call for property of infidel Jibr al-Dār al-Hamīdi 9th Shaʿbān - 26th June
134	36	ʿAsākir Abū-Kalām Complaint of abduction of son of al-Bashīr Daw al-Beit 14th Shaʿbān - 1st July
135	37	Beloved in God and believers in God Polished version of daʿwa and explanations of hadhra, Mahdīa and hijra 24th Rajab-16th Shaʿbān - 6th April-3rd July
139	38	Tribes of northern Darfur, especially al-Sheikh ʿAli walad Tāhir, etc. [Version of Letter 37, for specific audience] 24th Rajab-16th Shaʿbān - 6th April-3rd July

Volume 1

Page	No.	Recipient – Subject matter - Dates
		1299 - 1882
144	39	Mūsa Muhammad al-Ahmar Status of Mahdi and mobilisation for hijra 16th Sha'bān - 3rd July
148	40	'Asākir Abū-Kalām Complaint of faqi al-'Atāya about theft of 73 cows by 'Asākir's men 22nd Sha'bān - 9th July
149	41	Ahmad al-Badri and his brethren Call to join him in Jabal Gadīr 26th Sha'bān - 13th July
151	42	al-Amīn al-Darīr Reply explaining da'wa and Mahdi's status, urging migration 28th Sha'bān - 15th July
155	43	Muhammad al-Dādādi Repeats call to join hijra 28th Sha'bān - 15th July
157	44	Ahmad al-Badri and brethren Update on hijra and repeats call to join him Sha'bān - 18th June-16th July
159	45	al-Sheikh 'Abd-al-Rasūl, al-Sheikh Suleimān, etc. Call to join him in Jabal Gadīr Sha'bān - 18th June-16th July
162	46	Muhammad al-Amīn, son of Yūsuf al-Hindi [holy man in Jazīra] Appointment as deputy to accept pledges of allegiance Sha'bān - 18th June-16th July

Volume 1

Page	No.	Recipient – Subject matter - Dates
		1299 - 1882
165	47	ʿAsākir Abū-Kalām and others Further complaint of faqi al-ʿAtāya about theft of cows 3rd Ramadan - 29th July
166	48	Muhammad al-Raqīq Imminent attack on al-ʿObeid; call to join at al-Birka despite heavy rain 26th Ramadan - 14th August
168	49	People of Jebel al-Kadarū [and other Nuba Mountain areas] Appointment of ʿOmar, son of Mek ʿAdam, as amīr [general] 12th Shawwāl - 27th August
169	50	Respected beloved [dignitaries of al-ʿObeid], including al-Sheikh Bireir Reproach of ignoring daʿwa; obduracy of authorities Before 16th Shawwāl - before 31st August
174	51	People of al-ʿObeid [Copy of Letter 50] Before 16th Shawwāl - before 31st August
175	52	All the ʿulamāʾ, traders, sheikhs, etc. of al-ʿObeid Status as Khalīfa of Prophet Muhammad; hostile role of the ʿulamāʾ 16th Shawwāl - 31st August

Volume 1

Page	No.	Recipient – Subject matter - Dates
		1299 - 1882
179	53	All his beloved in God "Imām of the Century" on decline of irreligious and unjust Turkīa After 24th Shawwāl - after 8th September
183	54	al-Mak ʿOmar ʿAdam Praise for jihād in Nuba Mountains 15th Dhū al-Qaʿda - 28th September
184	55	The Tamām tribe [of ʿOmar ʿAdam] Appointment of ʿOmar ʿAdam as amīr in Nuba Mountains 15th Dhū al-Qaʿda - 28th September
185	56	Muhammad al-Dādādi Courteous welcome to ranks of Ansār Dhū al-Qaʿda - 14th Sept-13th Oct
186	57	Muhammad Jubāra, his friends and companions Commiseration on death of Ahmad Jubāra [Qādi al-Islām] at al-ʿObeid Dhū al-Qaʿda - 14th Sept-13th Oct
189	58	Taha al-Bashīr Urges application of Sharīʿa and Sunna and rejection of legal schools 2nd Dhū al-Hijja - 15th October
191	59	All the tribes of the western Dār Muhārib and their kin Mūsa Ahmad al-Bashīr al-Khanfari to be regional amīr 5th Dhū al-Hijja - 18th October

Volume 1

Page	No.	Recipient – Subject matter - Dates
		1299 - 1882
193	60	al-Hāj Marzūq and all his beloved Scolding for not joining Ansār; describes victory over Yūsuf al-Shallāli 17th Dhū al-Hijja - 30th October
195	61	All his beloved in God Call to fight Turks; fatwa not to enslave free women 21st Dhū al-Hijja - 3rd November
198	62	al-Sheikh Suleimān [Version of Letter 17] [During 1299] – 23rd Nov 1881-11th Nov 1882
200	63	ʿAsākir Abū-Kalām Requests confirmation of allegiance; final warning on misbehaviour [During 1299] – 23rd Nov 1881-11th Nov 1882
201	64	Ahmad al-Badri and his brethren Call to return stolen bulls [During 1299] – 23rd Nov 1881-11th Nov 1882
202	65	Ahmad Baqādi and those with him from the Ansār family License as deputy to gather clans and kill Turks [During 1299] – 23rd Nov 1881-11th Nov 1882
206	66	[Various tribes] in al-Fasher region Ahmad ibn al-Hāj Muhammad Zein al-ʿAbdīn as deputy [During 1299] – 23rd Nov 1881-11th Nov 1882

Volume 1

Page	No.	Recipient – Subject matter – Dates
		1299 – 1881-2
209	67	al-Sheikh Bābikr Saʿīd and al-Sheikh Ahmad ibn al-Hāj Bābikr General call to join Mahdīa [During 1299] – 23rd Nov 1881-11th Nov 1882
210	68	Fallāta tribes and those from tribes in al-Fasher region Summons to Jebel Gadīr [During 1299] – 23rd Nov 1881-11th Nov 1882
212	69	Hayāt ibn Saʿīd [in northern Nigeria] Details of Mahdīa hierarchy and call to hijra [During 1299] – 23rd Nov 1881-11th Nov 1882
216	70	[From] Hayāt ibn Saʿīd Reply, affirming faith in Mahdi and swearing allegiance [During 1299] – 23rd Nov 1881-11th Nov 1882
221	71	[No recipient identified] Prophet's instruction to change name to "Muhammad al-Mahdi" [During 1299] – 23rd Nov 1881-11th Nov 1882
		1300
222	72	al-Bashīr Nūr al-Dāʿim and those with him Call to join Ansār and select local leader 8th Muharram – 19th November
225	73	Khalīfa ʿAbdullāhi Order to discipline Ansār stealing cloaks and humiliating people 20th Muharram – 1st December

Volume 1

Page	No.	Recipient – Subject matter – Dates
		1300 – 1882
226	74	Mahmūd ʿAbd-al-Qādir Faqi ʿIsa of Beni Hamīd to be amīr; plans for assault on al-ʿObeid 5th Safar - 16th December
228	75	All the beloved, faithful adherents to him in the [Nuba] Mountains Mahmūd ʿAbd-al-Qādir mobilising for jihād at Jebel Fungur and Fashoda 5th Safar - 16th December
230	76	Mahmūd ʿAbd-al-Qādir and the Ansār with him Ansār should return stolen property; reduction of dowries 5th Safar - 16th December
232	77	ʿAbdallah al-Sanūssi Note on Ahmad Manūfal, ʿAbd-al-Rahmān al-Nujūmi and siege of Bāra After 7th Safar - after 18th December
234	78	All mayors and sheikhs of Harāyna and Qorʿān [in eastern Kordofan] Summons to discuss trouble with Ahmad Manūfal After 7th Safar - after 18th December
		1883
235	79	Mahmūd ʿAbd-al-Qādir Instructs enforcement of slave transaction 2nd Rabīʿ I - 11th January
236	80	Rulers, officers and natives of al-ʿObeid Final call on al-ʿObeid garrison to surrender 6th Rabīʿ I - 15th January

Volume 1

Page	No.	Recipient – Subject matter - Dates
		1300 – 1883
237	81	All God's people Clarification of Khalīfa 'Abdullāhi's status, titles and powers 17th Rabī' I - 27th January
242	82	al-Hāj Marzūq Permission to raise banner as local imām of Ansār 17th Rabī' I - 27th January
244	83	Easterners whose property was stolen in Kordofan Pledge to have looted goods restored; Ahmad Suleimān to monitor 1st Rabī' II - 9th February
245	84	'Asākir Abū-Kalām Sending Ahmad al-Badri to monitor behaviour 2nd Rabī' II - 10th February
246	85	All the tribes of Harāyna, al-Qur'ān and Ma'āqila Appointment of 'Abdallah al-Sanūssi as local leader 14th Rabī' II - 22nd February
248	86	al-Zubeir al-Fahl, Sāti Ahmad and others Condensed "Da'wa Proclamation" [see Letters 21 and 37] 24th Rabī' II - 4th March
249	87	All the khulafā', the umarā', his followers and supporters of religion General pep-talk and reminder of core values 26th Rabī' II - 6th March

Volume 1

Page	No.	Recipient – Subject matter - Dates
		1300 – 1883
254	88	Ibrāhīm Dāwi Asks old school-friend from al-Ghobosh why he hasn't joined him 28th Rabīʿ II - 8th March
258	89	Muhammad ibn Ahmad Dafaʾallah Rewards revelation of father's cache of money with women and horses Rabīʿ II - 9th Feb-9th March
260	90	Muhammad ibn al-Hāj Ahmad Mahdi devotes himself to religion and devolving responsibility 11th Jumāda I - 20th March
262	91	The beloved, the faithful and believers in one God General pep-talk on virtues of jihād and rallying-call 12th Jumāda I - 21st March
265	92	His beloved in God Organisation of forces under banners 13th Jumāda I - 22nd March
268	93	al-Manna Ismāʿīl Constant complaints about thieving Jawāmʿa followers Before 25th Jumāda I - before 3rd April
272	94	al-Manna Ismāʿīl Notice of recipient's replacement as local leader 25th Jumāda I - 3rd April

Volume 1

Page	No.	Recipient – Subject matter - Dates
		1300 – 1883
274	95	All the Zaghāwa and their neighbours [in Darfur] Call to reform behaviour, explaining core Muslim values 25th Jumāda I - 3rd April
278	96	All his beloved in God and believers in God [Version of Letter 95 for more general audience] 25th Jumāda I - 3rd April
283	97	All his companions, followers and aides Allocation of all assets to Beit al-Māl under Ahmad Suleimān Jumāda I - 10th March-8th Apr
285	98	Muhammad [al-Taweim] the "Praise-Singer" General letter urging loyalty to Mahdīa Jumāda I - 10th March-8th Apr
286	99	'Omar Ilyās, Muhammadein al-'Areiq, and those with them Virtues of fund-raising for military 13th Jumāda II - 21st April
288	100	All the khulafā' and umarā' Ban on use of firearms; to be stored under Khalīfa 'Abdullāhi 13th Jumāda II - 21st April
290	101	al-Manna Ismā'īl Ultimatum to join Mahdīa as a subordinate within four days 17th Jumāda II - 25th April

Volume 1

Page	No.	Recipient – Subject matter – Dates
		1300 – 1883
292	102	Followers of ʿAttā al-Manān al-Suleihābi Order to fight enemies of God 25th Jumāda II - 3rd May
294	103	ʿAttā al-Manān al-Suleihābi Order to detain and punish raiders who had attacked Ansār families After 25th Jumāda II - after 3rd May
296	104	All his beloved [including people of Suakin and al-ʿObeid] Reply, ordering them to serve under ʿAbdullāhi wad al-Nūr Jumāda II - 9th Apr-7th May
298	105	The applicant Reply, observing that ordeals and risks are part of joining the Mahdīa Jumāda II - 9th Apr-7th May
299	106	Mahmūd ʿAbd-al-Qādir Request to take care of Sheikh al-Qurāshi 22nd Jum I or Jum II - 31st Apr or 30th May
300	107	All the umarā' and officials, especially the Qādi al-Islam Order to drop claims pre-12 Rajab 1299 [30 May 1882], with exceptions Before Rajab - before 9th May
301	108	All the sheikhs of the Faith, the umarā' and their deputies Social ordinances, listing specific offences and their penalties Before Rajab - before 9th May

Volume 1

Page	No.	Recipient – Subject matter – Dates
		1300 – 1883
309	109	The Birashāriyīn, the Shāb Dīnāb and the Hadendawa of Tāka Reproach for lateness in joining Mahdīa 1st Rajab - 8th May
315	110	al-Tayyib ibn Muhammad al-Tayyib al-Majdhūb and all the Jaʿāliyīn [Version of Letter 109 for specific audience, related to ʿOsmān Digna] 1st Rajab - 8th May
319	111	The populace of Suakin Call to fight "Turks" under ʿOsmān Digna 1st Rajab - 8th May
322	112	The populace of the suburbs of Suakin Call to besiege Suakin under ʿOsmān Digna 1st Rajab - 8th May
326	113	Ibrāhīm Muhammad Dhaw and his followers [Version of Letter 50, adapted for eastern audience] After 1st Rajab - after 8th May
329	114	His beloved in God and believers in God and his Book Extols benefits of Mahdīa; warning about fate of Sheikh al-Manna Ismāʿīl 4th Rajab - 11th May
334	115	Muhammad al-Mahdi al-Sanūssi Appoints al-Sanūssi as third khalīfa and urges migration or jihād 5th Rajab - 12th May

Volume 1

Page	No.	Recipient – Subject matter – Dates
		1300 – 1883
340	116	Muhammad al-Mahdi al-Sanūssi [Version of Letter 115, including parts of "Daʿwa Proclamation"] 5th Rajab - 12th May
343	117	ʿAbdallāhi al-Khalīfa and al-Shāmi Abū-Safīa Announces intention to move east; order to inventory loot and join him 8th Rajab - 15th May
345	118	Ahmad al-Badri Summons in the face of advance by General Hicks 16th Rajab - 23rd May
347	119	Mahmūd walad al-Khabīr Call to join Ansār when he reaches the White Nile 18th Rajab - 25th May
349	120	The supporters of al-Manna Ismāʿīl Reply, chiding them for bad behaviour, urging renewed allegiance After 4th Rajab - after 11th May
356	121	All the khulafāʾ and umarāʾ, their deputies and supporters of the Faith Bring all loot from capture of Bāra to Khalīfa ʿAbdullāhi 24th Rajab - 31st May
358	122	ʿAbdallah al-Nūr Permits him to lead prayers wherever he is 23rd Rajab - 30th May

Volume 1

Page	No.	Recipient – Subject matter - Dates
		1300 – 1883
359	123	Traders in al-ʿObeid market Criticism for dishonest trading 23rd Rajab - 30th May
361	124	The Ashrāf Call to obey commanders in jihād 6th Ramadan - 11th July
363	125	Hayāt ibn Saʿīd Reply to descendant of Usman Dan Fodio, welcoming allegiance to Mahdīa 2nd Shawwāl - 6th August
367	126	Muhammad al-Sirāj ibn Muhammad al-Nūr Reply to wandering holy man, urging him to join 12th Shawwāl - 15th August
369	127	Muhammad al-Malīkān and al-Hāj Marzūq Delegating letter of complaint for resolution 18th Shawwāl - 21st August
370	128	Khalīfa ʿAbdullāhi Order to punish people who attacked Ansār despite Mahdi's laissez-passer 29th Shawwāl - 2nd September
371	129	Muhammad al-Raqīq Advice to follow path of piety and join Mahdīa 3rd Dhū al-Qaʿda - 5th September
373	130	Chiefs of the Rizeigāt Appointment of Muhammad al-Raqīq as amīr 3rd Dhū al-Qaʿda - 5th September

Volume 1

Page	No.	Recipient – Subject matter - Dates
		1300 – 1883
375	131	People of the areas of Bāra and al-'Obeid Marital status of couples who separate to serve the Mahdīa 13th Dhū al-Qa'da - 15th September
377	132	Khalīfa 'Abdullāhi Ban on luxuries, including food, drink and furnishings 18th Dhū al-Qa'da - 29th September
379	133	'Abd-al-Rahmān Mansūr, Muhammad 'Abdallah, etc. Reiteration of Mahdīa's principles, calls for immediate hijra Dhū al-Qa'da - 3rd Sept-2nd Oct
381	134	al-Sadīq al-Hāj Ahmad Hadhra and others Praise for support and calls for hijra Dhū al-Qa'da - 3rd Sept-2nd Oct
383	135	'Ali ibn al-Amīn al-Darīr [Refers to Letter 42, to recipient's father] 10th Dhū al-Hijja - 12th October
384	136	Ahmad al-Makāshfi Short note, accepting recipient's will 10th Dhū al-Hijja - 12th October
385	137	His beloved in God and his followers Warns of perils of the world and some corrupt followers 10th Dhū al-Hijja - 12th October

Volume 1

Page	No.	Recipient – Subject matter - Dates
		1300 – 1883
389	138	His beloved and his followers on the path of God's prophet Advantages of jihād, promise of total victory 29th Dhū al-Hijja - 31st October
393	139	His beloved ones who join the hijra and jihād Warns against hoarding money; poor recruits taken care of by Beit al-Māl 14th Dhū al-Hijja - 16th October
395	140	All his beloved in God Indication that other holy men may lead people to God 15th Dhū al-Hijja - 17th October
397	141	His beloved people of the banners Call to stop use of musical instruments except military drums 17th Dhū al-Hijja - 19th October
399	142	His beloved in God General moral lecture, including proper behaviour in mosques 18th Dhū al-Hijja - 20th October
401	143	His beloved in God Bans unsheathing or waving of weapons and riding in inhabited areas 18th Dhū al-Hijja - 20th October
403	144	Khalīfa 'Abdullāhi Send battalions to monitor progress of Hicks without pitched battle Before 29th Dhū al-Hijja - before 31st October

Volume 1

Page	No.	Recipient – Subject matter – Dates
		1300 – 1883
404	145	Officers and troops of the Hicks Pasha expedition Ultimatum: surrender or death 29th Dhū al-Hijja - 31st October
406	146	Muhammad 'Osmān Abū-Girja and 'Omar Ilyās and Rahma Manūfal Ban on looting; harrying skirmishes instead of pitched battles 19th Dhū al-Hijja - 21st October
408	147	His beloved and his aides Order to leave administration to umarā' and their deputies 20th Dhū al-Hijja - 22nd October
410	148	All the beloved Muslims Order to refer claims of injustice to khulafā' or umarā' Dhū al-Hijja - 3rd-31st October
411	149	Muhammad al-Badawi Abū-Safīya Public decree, ordering all claims of injustice to be filed without hesitation 24th Dhū al-Hijja - 29th October
413	150	Muhammad al-Taweim [the praise-singer] Moralistic reply to petition 26th Dhū al-Hijja - 31st October
417	151	Muhammad al-Taweim the Praise Singer Lecture on spiritual, not material, bonds [i.e. don't expect money] Dhū al-Hijja - 3rd-31st October

Volume 1

Page	No.	Recipient – Subject matter - Dates
		1300 – 1883
418	152	Ahmad Suleimān Warning of moral risks from great wealth [i.e. administering the Beit-al-Māl] Dhū al-Hijja - 3rd-31st October
420	153	Muhammad Sharīf Nūr al-Dā'im Call for immediate hijra, predicts destruction of Hicks expedition [During 1300] - 12th Nov 1882-1st Nov 1883
424	154	Muhammad al-Raqīq Orders him to get "Turks" to surrender and southern tribes to join Mahdīa [During 1300] - 12th Nov 1882-1st Nov 1883
426	155	Muhammad al-Hāj Ahmad Reply, welcoming expression of obedience [During 1300] - 12th Nov 1882-1st Nov 1883
427	156	Muhammad al-Hāj Ahmad Short general note on morality [During 1300] - 12th Nov 1882-1st Nov 1883
428	157	The religious police [subsequently the Khalīfa's corps of guards] Orders Ansār to obey the Mulazimīn in dictates of behaviour [During 1300] - 12th Nov 1882-1st Nov 1883
432	158	All the beloved Instructs reduction in wedding expenditure [During 1300] - 12th Nov 1882-1st Nov 1883

Volume 1

Page	No.	Recipient – Subject matter - Dates
		1300 – 1882-3
433	159	Abdallah al-Sanūssi Requests transfer of fifth of his loot to the Beit al-Māl [During 1300] - 12th Nov 1882-1st Nov 1883
434	160	The 'ulamā' of evil Lecture on corruption in their hearts, leading people astray [During 1300] - 12th Nov 1882-1st Nov 1883
436	161	Scribes of the Mahdīa's secretariat Instruction to adopt formal Ottoman style of letter-writing [During 1300] - 12th Nov 1882-1st Nov 1883
438	162	Khalīfa 'Abdullāhi Order to hand 100 rifles to Syrian officer leading Jawāma'a tribe into battle [During 1300] - 12th Nov 1882-1st Nov 1883
439	163	'Attā al-Manān al-Suleihābi and his companions Appendix [possibly to Letter 103] on division of reclaimed loot [During 1300] - 12th Nov 1882-1st Nov 1883
440	164	'Attā al-Manān al-Suleihābi and others Reply, identifying those who had robbed the Ansār families [see Letter 103] [During 1300] - 12th Nov 1882-1st Nov 1883
443	165	Muhammad al-Taweim Decision relating to a case of marital dowry [During 1300] - 12th Nov 1882-1st Nov 1883

Volume 1

Page	No.	Recipient – Subject matter – Dates
		1300 – 1882-3
444	166	Khalīfa 'Abdullāhi Pardons Khalīfa's relatives for attacking Ashrāf, orders their release [During 1300] - 12th Nov 1882-1st Nov 1883
446	167	Khalīfa 'Abdullāhi Rules for testimony and punishment in cases of sexual offences [During 1300] - 12th Nov 1882-1st Nov 1883
447	168	All the beloved in God General notes on aims and taboos of Mahdīa; repeats ban on old legal cases [During 1300] - 12th Nov 1882-1st Nov 1883
451	169	The Halāwiyīn peoples [in the Jazīra region] Appointment of Muhammad al-Tayyib al-Basīr as local amīr [During 1300] - 12th Nov 1882-1st Nov 1883
454	170	All the tribes of Duweih [in western Sudan] Appointment of Ibrāhīm Ahmad Zerrūq as local amīr [During 1300] - 12th Nov 1882-1st Nov 1883
457	171	The [western] clans of the Harāyana, Tureifīa, Sureihāt and Hiyādīa Rebuke for abandoning jihād and disobeying orders [During 1300] - 12th Nov 1882-1st Nov 1883
459	172	Ahmad Jafūn Order to track Hicks expedition and report movements [During 1300] - 12th Nov 1882-1st Nov 1883

Volume 1

Page	No.	Recipient – Subject matter – Dates
		1300 – 1882-3
461	173	[From al-Hāj Abd-al-Qādir] Graphic description of vision of the Mahdi conquering Mecca [During 1300 - 12th Nov 1882-1st Nov 1883

Volume 2

Vol 2		126 letters (4th November 1883 - 29th April 1884)
Page	No.	Recipient – Subject matter - Dates

1301 - 1883

Page	No.	
1	174	Hamid al-Nīl Hāmid Reply, on how to perform communal prayers 3rd Muharram - 4th November
2	175	ʿAbd-al-Samad Sharfi Notifies deputy at Dārā that Hicks is approaching 5th Muharram - 6th November
9	176	His beloved in God, the umarāʾ, al-muqādīm [section leaders] and their units Call to bring loot to al-Birka for division according to Sharīʿa 5th Muharram - 6th November
12	177	All the umarāʾ, muqādīm and their subordinates Rebuke about inefficiency in collecting weapons and obeying Khalīfa 5th Muharram - 6th November
13	178	Muhammad Sālih Suwār al-Dahab Prepare two camels to carry ammunition looted from Hicks After 5th Muharram - after 6th November
14	179	al-Hāja Zeina daughter of al-Sheikh Sālih and her [female] relatives Reply, commendation on endurance after martyrdom of husband 7th Muharram - 8th November

Volume 2

Page	No.	Recipient – Subject matter – Dates
		1301 – 1883
16	180	All his beloved ones in God, his umarā', muqādīm and others Banning firearms in inhabited areas or on the march; severe punishments 7th Muharram – 8th November
18	181	All the umarā', muqādīm and their subordinates Denounces looting for personal enrichment 9th Muharram – 10th November
19	182	His beloved in God / To whom it may concern in Khartoum Order to tighten siege of Khartoum until his arrival 10th Muharram – 11th November
21	183	Muhammad Khālid Zughul Advice on appointment as amīr of Darfur 10th Muharram – 11th November
23	184	The peoples of Darfur Call for collective jihād under his agent Muhammad Khālid Zughul 10th Muharram – 11th November
26	185	His beloved and all his followers Ethical advice on humility; restrictions on riding horses 12th or 21st Muharram – 13th or 22nd November
29	186	His beloved Ban on canvassing for official positions 12th Muharram – 13th November

Volume 2

Page	No.	Recipient – Subject matter – Dates
		1301 - 1883
32	187	Abū-Bakr Jaʿfar al-Mīrghani Reply, criticising attitude and determined resistance [of Khatmīa] to Mahdīa 13th Muharram - 14th November
35	188	[From Ahmad Suleimān] Brigade of al-Sharīf Suleimān al-ʿUbeid less than recorded strength 27th Muharram - 28th November
37	189	Ahmad Suleimān Reply to Letter 188, ordering instruction in proper record-keeping After 27th Muharram - after 28th November
38	190	[From ʿAbdallah al-Nūr] Request for instructions on handling loot remaining at al-Birka 28th Muharram - 1st December
40	191	ʿAbdallah al-Nūr Reply to Letter 190, rebuking recipient for asking about secret plans 28th Muharram - 1st December
41	192	Ahmad Jafūn Move with Asākir's forces to besiege al-Mak ʿAdam at Jebel Tagali 4th Safar - 5th December
43	193	His beloved pursuers of God's path Prisoners should accept their fate as decreed 5th Safar - 6th December

Volume 2

Page	No.	Recipient – Subject matter – Dates
		1301 – 1883
45	194	[From ʿAbdallah al-Nūr] Questions about status of women in Bārā, married to "Turks" or Ansār 28th Muharram – 29th November
46	195	ʿAbdallah al-Nūr Reply to Letter 194, clarifying different matrimonial rules under Sharīʿa 5th Safar – 6th December
47	196	His beloved in God Ban on asking questions about future strategy or tactics 5th Safar – 6th December
49	197	All his beloved and followers Long moral preamble; ban on hiding loot 6th Safar – 7th December
57	198	Khalīl Hussein and his aforementioned brothers Reply, alloting times to attend public audience 6th Safar – 7th December
58	199	Muhammad ʿOsmān ibn al-Sayyid al-Hassan al-Mīrghani Rebuke about disbelief in Mahdīa; order to join him or alternative amīr 14th Safar – 15th December
60	200	The Beni Hussein tribes and the sons of the ʿOweidha Refers to fighting between them, urging good treatment of prisoners 23rd Safar – 24th December

Volume 2

Page	No.	Recipient – Subject matter – Dates
		1301 - 1883
62	201	All the Siyāq [Muslims resident in the south] On relations with non-Muslim southern tribes, e.g. the Shilluk 23rd Safar - 24th December
64	202	[From Ahmad Suleimān to his assistants in the Beit al-Māl] Call for diligence and sincerity 26th Safar - 27th December
66	203	All those who obey and listen Endorses Ahmad Suleiman's call [Letter 202], adding further instructions 26th Safar - 27th December
67	204	al-ʿUbeid Badr Order to accept local leadership of Muhammad al-Tayyib al-Basīr After Safar - December 1883-February 1884
70	205	His beloved, especially Dafaʾallah the disciple of al-ʿUbeid Badr Call to besiege Khartoum [from the north-east] under al-ʿUbeid Badr After Safar - December 1883-February 1884
71	206	Muhammad al-Tāhir ibn al-Tayyib Qamr al-Dīn al-Majdhūb Call to join ʿOsmān Digna; note on status of martyred leaders 1st or 11th Rabīʿ I - 31st Dec 1883 or 10th Jan 1884

Volume 2

Page	No.	Recipient – Subject matter - Dates
		1301 - 1884
74	207	His beloved and his companions General moral prescriptions for life under new order 2nd Rabīʿ I - 1st January
78	208	All the nomads and tribes of Suakin Call to join jihād under ʿOsmān Digna 9th Rabīʿ I - 8th January
81	209	ʿOsmān Digna Call to reply on God and small elite force rather than mass support 10th Rabīʿ I - 9th January
86	210	ʿOsmān Digna Rebuke at lack of progress reports; late notification of Hicks' defeat 10th Rabīʿ I - 9th January
90	211	al-Sadīq al-Hāj Ahmad Hadhra and his brothers Rebuke at delay and urges hijra or jihād in their own [unknown] location 21st Rabīʿ I - 20th January
91	212	[From unnamed legal officers of the Mahdīa] Six specific questions on family law, e.g. slander, inheritance, etc. 25th Rabīʿ I - 24th January
92	213	Legal officers of the Mahdīa Reply to Letter 212, giving detailed answers 25th Rabīʿ I - 24th January

Volume 2

Page	No.	Recipient – Subject matter – Dates
		1301 – 1884
97	214	His brothers in God General moral advice Before 27th Rabīʿ I - before 26th January
100	215	Khalīfa ʿAbdullāhi Order to bring seventy men from each brigade for ritual purification 27th Rabīʿ I - 26th January
101	216	His belowed in God and his followers/ʿAbd-al-Samad Sharfi Precepts on morality [as preached to the groups of seventy] 27th Rabīʿ I - 26th January
115	217	ʿAbd-al-Samad Sharfi and his brothers, ʿOmar Ilyās and his brothers Reply to letter on fall of Dārā, appointing him interim commander there 28th Rabīʿ I - 27th January
118	218	Muhammad Khālid Zughul Pardon for family of named individual killed at al-Fasher; transfer to Mahdi 29th Rabīʿ I - 28th January
119	219	[From Hassīb and Hāshim] Request for appointment as umarāʿ to the Zaghāwa [During 1301] - 2nd Nov 1883-20th Oct 1884

Volume 2

Page	No.	Recipient – Subject matter - Dates
		1301 - 1884
120	220	Muhammad Khālid Zughul Reply to Letter 219, agreeing to appointment of Hassīb 29th Rabīʿ I - 28th January
121	221	al-ʿUbeid Bacr Rebuke for delays and call for hijra or join siege of Khartoum Rabīʿ I - 31st Dec 1883-29th Jan 1884
124	222	Awad al-Karīm Ahmad Abū-Sinn and his people Reply, urging him to disobey the "Turks" and stop attacking the Batāhīn Rabīʿ I - 31st Dec 1883-29th Jan 1884
127	223	Awad al-Karīm Ahmad Abū-Sinn and his people Orders him to join Muhammad al-Tayyib al-Basīr Rabīʿ I - 31st Dec 1883-29th Jan 1884
130	224	Sālih al-Mak Urges his to rebel against his employers and join the movement Rabīʿ I - 31st Dec 1883-29th Jan 1884
134	225	Muhammad al-Tayyib al-Basīr Personal advice on modest comportment of a leader Rabīʿ I - 31st Dec 1883-29th Jan 1884
137	226	Muhammad al-Tayyib al-Basīr Refers complaint by ʿAbd-al-Jabbār ibn al-Sheikh Nūr al-Dāʿim Rabīʿ I - 31st Dec 1883-29th Jan 1884

Volume 2

Page	No.	Recipient – Subject matter - Dates
		1301 – 1883-4

138   227   Muhammad al-Tayyib al-Basīr
            Asks to take care of family of al-Sheikh al-Tayyib
            and al-Sheikh Nūr al-Dā'im
            Rabī' I - 31st Dec 1883-29th Jan 1884

141   228   al-Qurāshi al-Tayyib al-Basīr
            Notification of complaint against him [see Letter
            226]
            Rabī' I - 31st Dec 1883-29th Jan 1884

142   229   'Abd-al-Jabbār Nūr al-Dā'im
            Warns that guilty face hudūd punishment; Mahdi
            coming to Khartoum
            Rabī' I - 31st Dec 1883-29th Jan 1884

144   230   To whom it may concern
            Award of flock of sheep and slaves to widow and
            orphans in Jebel al-Harāza
            before Rabī' II - before 30th January

145   231   [No recipient identified]
            Pledge that army of "Turks", however numerous,
            will be defeated
            1st Rabī' II - 30th January

147   232   Muhammad al-Tayyib al-Basīr
            Description of hadhra; promise to send 100 rifles
            but no artillery
            6th Rabī' II - 4th February

150   233   His beloved
            Commentary of verse from Qur'ān [Sūrat Yūnus,
            10/25]
            9th Rabī' II - 7th February

Volume 2

Page	No.	Recipient – Subject matter – Dates
		1301 – 1884
153	234	Hayāt ibn Saʿīd Third letter [see Letters 69 and 125], mentions letters to two other western leaders 11th Rabīʿ II - 9th February
156	235	Muhammad al-Tayyib al-Suleihābi Discussion of loot; Abū-Rof clan criticised for asking for government help 13th Rabīʿ II - 11th February
158	236	To Rawāwiqa nomads Refers to complaints by local amīr, urges propriety of dress and behaviour 16th Rabīʿ II - 14th February
160	237	Nomads residing in Shilluk areas Praise for Shilluk loyalty; urges hospitality and postponement of disputes 18th Rabīʿ II - 16th February
162	238	Ansār and nomads frequenting the al-Namā mountains Call to abandon pagan practises; al-Sheikh al-ʿUbeid confirmed as local amīr 20th Rabīʿ II - 18th February
165	239	ʿAbd-al-Samad Sharfi Permissibility of legal claims following surrender to Mahdi or specific victories 22nd Rabīʿ II - 20th February

Volume 2

Page	No.	Recipient – Subject matter – Dates
		1301 – 1884
167	240	al-Sayyid Muhammad ibn al-Sayyid Musāʿid and all the Ashrāf Orders jihād under al-Kheir Khojali, ʿOsmān Digna or the Mahdi himself 23rd Rabīʿ II – 21st February
169	241	al-Sharīf Ahmad, al-Bashīr Muhammad and all the natives of Atbara Rebuke for delay; orders jihād under local amīr al-Hussein ʿAbd-al-Wāhid 27th Rabīʿ II – 25th February
172	242	al-Mak ʿAdam ʿOmar Flattering letter referring to opposition to Khalīfa ʿAbdullāhi, orders apology Rabīʿ II – 20th Jan-27th Feb
174	243	All his beloved in God General moral pep-talk Rabīʿ II – 20th Jan-27th Feb
179	244	All the umarāʿ, deputies, admistrators and all their supporters Clarification of finances: from Beit al-Māl, self-financing and from loot Rabīʿ II – 20th Jan-27th Feb
184	245	al-Amīn al-Darīr Refers to earlier correspondence [see Letter 42] and urges immediate migration Rabīʿ II – 20th Jan-27th Feb

Volume 2

Page	No.	Recipient – Subject matter - Dates
		1301 – 1884
188	246	To his relatives and his beloved Rebuke to closest family and followers for lack of faith in him Rabīʿ II - 20th Jan-27th Feb
190	247	His beloved in God and his followers Long, carefully-drafted letter on importance of prayer and proper behaviour Rabīʿ II - 20th Jan-27th Feb
209	248	Muhammad al-Kheir ʿAbdallah Khojali Urges former tutor to join jihād either in Berber or with Mahdi Rabīʿ II - 20th Jan-27th Feb
212	249	Mayors and dignitaries of al-ʿObeid Call to give money for the jihād and prepare themselves Rabīʿ II - 20th Jan-27th Feb
214	250	Muhammad al-Tayyib al-Basīr Reply, annulling a pre-Mahdīa divorce Rabīʿ I or II - 31st Dec 1883-29th Jan 1884
216	251	Halāwiyīn dignitaries ʿAbd-al-Rahmān al-Qurāshi, etc. Refers to letter to [Sheikh] al-ʿUbeid wad Badr and attack on Khartoum Before Jumāda I - before 28th February
218	252	Muhammad Khālid Zughul and those with him Praise for conquest of Darfur; call to distribute his proclamations and Rātib 3rd or 4th Jumāda I - 2nd or 3rd March

Volume 2

Page	No.	Recipient – Subject matter – Dates
		1301 – 1884
221	253	Muhammad Khālid Zughul Allocation of loot by percentage, except weaponry, horses and Jihādīa troops 3rd Jumāda I - 2nd March
223	254	Muhammad al-Tayyib al-Basīr General sermon on morality; warning not to accept bribes 3rd or 9th Jumāda I - 2nd or 8th March
226	255	Muhammad al-Tayyib al-Basīr Orders obedience to Muhammad ʿOsmān Abū-Girja, amīr of the Jazīra Before 4th Jumāda I - before 3rd March
228	256	Muhammad Khālid Zughul [with supplement] Comprehensive update on all campaigns currently underway 4th and 8th Jumāda I - 3th and 7th March
233	257	His beloved and his brothers General moral exhortations on compassion and contempt for this world 4th Jumāda I - 3rd March
238	258	al-Mak ʿAdam ʿOmar Explains reasons for jailing recipient [seizing Mahdi's property] After 4th Jumāda I - after 3rd March
240	259	Khalīfa ʿAbdullāhi Order to investigate those who failed to accompany Abū-Girja After 4th Jumāda I - after 3rd March

Volume 2

Page	No.	Recipient – Subject matter – Dates
		1301 – 1884
242	260	Muḥammad Sharīf Nūr al-Dāʿim Denies ordering seizure of recipient's property; affirms respect for former mentor 6th Jumāda I - 4th March
244	261	[From Gordon Pasha] Appointment as ruler of Sudan; offers sultanate of Kordofan 16th Rabīʿ II - 14th February
246	262	Gordon Pasha Reply to Letter 261, a point-by-point rejection of Gordon's statements 11th Jumāda I - 9th March
254	263	Gordon Pasha [first supplement] Note on enclosed gift of jibba 11th Jumāda I - 9th March
255	264	Gordon Pasha [second supplement] Urges careful translation and reading of main letter [Letter 262] 11th Jumāda I - 9th March
256	265	[From Ilyās Um Bireir to Gordon] Reasons for following the Mahdi; urges Gordon to do the same [No date]
258	266	[From Gordon Pasha] Reply to Letter 262, short and angry [No date]

Volume 2

Page	No.	Recipient – Subject matter – Dates
		1301 – 1884
259	267	Muhammad Khālid Zughul Order to crush rebellion of al-Tāhir al-Tījāni 12th Jumāda I - 10th March
261	268	Hassan ʿAbd-al-Karīm and those with him, etc. Appointment of al-Sirāj al-Hāj al-Daw as local amīr 15th Jumāda I - 13th March
263	269	All his beloved in God Women to be veiled and banned from public spaces unless very young or elderly 18th Jumāda I - 16th March
265	270	Sālih Fadlallah al-Kabāshi Reply, urging return of looted property to rightful owners 18th Jumāda I - 16th March
267	271	His beloved in God Sharīʿa to apply to all without discrimination 18th Jumāda I - 16th March
271	272	Mayors and dignitaries of al-Tureifīa Urged to hand over loot to Ahmad Muhammad al-Hāj Ahmad 18th Jumāda I - 16th March
273	273	ʿOsmān Digna Congratulations on victories; advice on how to treat shirkers and enemies 20th Jumāda I - 18th March

Volume 2

Page	No.	Recipient – Subject matter – Dates
		1301 – 1884
276	274	ʿOsmān Digna Rebuke for scarcity of correspondence; refers to captured government letters 20th Jumāda I - 18th March
279	275	ʿAli Muhammad al-Shinturābi [with supplement] Order to fight under local amīr Muhammad al-Kheir ʿAbdallah Khojali 28th Jum I and 1st Jum II - 27th and 28th March
283	276	[From Khalīfa ʿAli [wad] al-Helu] Query about division of the late Tātāī's property Jumāda I - 28th Feb-28th March
284	277	Khalīfa ʿAli al-Helu Reply to Letter 276, with answer on division according to God's law Jumāda I - 28th Feb-28th March
285	278	To his beloved [template format] Inhabitants of Khartoum suburbs ordered to pick amīr and besiege city Jumāda I - 28th Feb-28th March
288	279	To his beloved, his followers and companions Order for new recruits to read the Rātib regularly Jumāda I - 28th Feb-28th March
291	280	al-Jallāl Muhammad Sharīf Urging him to acknowledge guilt and accept punishment for alleged fornication After Jumāda II - after 29th March

42

Volume 2

Page	No.	Recipient – Subject matter - Dates
		1301 – 1884
294	281	Administrators of northern Nile regions, especially Abū-Girja Ordering respect for the Mahdi's companions and khulafā' Jumāda I-Ramadan - 28th Feb-25th June
296	282	Population of Salāmat al-Bāsha hamlet Notice of seizure of Dārā and Shakka and conversion of Rudolf Slatin 1st Jumāda II - 28th March
299	283	Hamid al-Nīl Hāmid General moral observations on sincere faith and the life hereafter 16th Jumāda II - 13th April
301	284	Mahmūd 'Abd-al-Gādir Advice to "Uncle" that the Mahdi is heading to Khartoum 17th Jumāda II - 14th April
302	285	Muhammad Yūsuf [Sultān of Barqu, west of Darfur] Refusal to call him "Sultān"; refers to letter to al-Sanūssi 19th Jumāda II - 16th April
309	286	Muhammad Yūsuf Thanks for gift of 500 riyāls; accompanies gift of jibba, banner, etc. 19th Jumāda II - 16th April
310	287	All the beloved Ban on label "darwīsh" 20th Jumāda II - 17th April

Volume 2

Page	No.	Recipient – Subject matter – Dates
		1301 – 1884
312	288	al-Sayyid Muḥammad Musāʿid, etc. Asks them to desert the "Turks" and fight under amīr Muḥammad al-Kheir 25th Jumāda II – 22nd April
316	289	The beloved Repeat of ban on label "darwīsh" [see Letter 287] Jumāda II – 29th March–26th April
317	290	His beloved Urges only the able-bodied to accompany him east to Khartoum Jumāda II – 29th March–26th April
319	291	His beloved in God Advises new appointees to co-operate with modesty and compassion Jumāda II – 29th March–26th April
323	292	Muḥammad ʿAli Qurāfi Restatement of reasons for Mahdīa; urges immediate hijra Jumāda II – 29th March–26th April
327	293	Suleimān Sāliḥ Notice of imminent departure for Khartoum; rendez-vous at al-Rahad or Shurkeila Jumāda II – 29th March–26th April
328	294	All his beloved and followers Repeat of ban on label "darwīsh" [see Letters 287 and 289] Before 20th Jumāda II – before 17th April

44

Volume 2

Page	No.	Recipient – Subject matter – Dates
		1301 – 1884
329	295	Mahmūd 'Abd-al-Qādir Order to round up large body of deserters currently at Jebel al-Harāza 27th Jumāda I or II – 25th Mar or 24th Apr
330	296	[From Khalīfa 'Abdullāhi] Sent two colleagues to his father's grave; asks the Mahdi if he can go instead After Jumāda II – after 29th April
332	297	Khalīfa 'Abdullāhi Reply, denying permission, suggesting he read the fatiha from afar After Jumāda II – after 29th April
333	298	To the beloved, especially Khalīfa 'Abdullāhi Orders beheading of a companion named Dūka for immorality After Jumāda II – after 29th April
335	299	Muhammad al-Tayyib al-Basīr Reassures him that he is not to be subordinated to Sāleh al-Mak After Jumāda II – after 29th April

Volume 3

Vol 3		153 letters (27th April 1884 - 20th October 1884)
Page	No.	Recipient – Subject matter - Dates
		1301 - 1884
1	300	The Ansār beseiging Khartoum Order to tighten siege and not squabble over food supplies 1st Rajab - 27th April
6	301	Those besiging Khartoum Praise for unity and diligence but rules out distribution of loot 1st Rajab - 27th April
19	302	His beloved in God's way and his helpers Calls for stamina in the face of problems; rules out distribution of loot After 1st Rajab - after 27th April
29	303	Son, brothers and kin of al-Malik ʿAbd-al-Rahmān Condolences on death of al-Malik ʿAbd-al-ahmān, order to choose successor 3rd Rajab - 29th April
31	304	The beloved Order not to grieve for martyrs 3rd Rajab - 29th April
33	305	[From Idrīs Ahmad Hāshmi] Query on legitimacy of marriage to woman breast-fed by same wet-nurse 7th Rajab - 3rd May
34	306	Idrīs Ahmad Hāshmi Reply, prohibiting marriage between two people fed at the same breast 7th Rajab - 3rd May

Volume 3

Page	No.	Recipient – Subject matter – Dates
		1301 – 1884
35	307	Idrīs Ahmad Hāshmi [Copy of Letter 306] 7th Rajab - 3rd May
36	308	Ahmad Saʿad the Praise Singer Reply, authorising songs in praise of the Prophet and the Mahdi 9th Rajab - 5th May
37	309	Mahmūd ʿAbd-al-Qādir Appointment of Muhammad al-Badawi Abi Safīya in Tagali region Before 12th Rajab - before 8th May
38	310	Mahmūd ʿAbd-al-Qādir Endorsement of pardon for Abū-Khumsmāʿa on condition of obedience 21st Rajab - 17th May
40	311	al-Sheikh Ahmad al-Jaʿali and family, followers and companions Expectations of support from distinguished family and call for jihād After 22nd Rajab - after 18th May
43	312	Muhammad al-Kheir ʿAbdallah Khojali Authority to make appointments in wake of conquest of Berber district After 22nd Rajab - after 18th May
46	313	Ansār with Muhammad al-Kheir ʿAbdallah Khojali Thanks for support given to Muhammad al-Kheir After 22nd Rajab - after 18th May

Volume 3

Page	No.	Recipient – Subject matter – Dates
		1301 – 1884
48	314	Muhammad al-Kheir 'Abdallah Khojali Choice of Muhammad Ahmad al-Karīf or Ahmad Hamza to be amīr of Shendi After 22nd Rajab - after 18th May
50	315	'Osmān Digna Praise for victories and authority to make administrative appointments 23rd Rajab - 19th May
54	316	Muhammad walad Hamid, amīr of the Shukrīa on the Atbara River Reply to letter re. mutiny of Hadendawa fighters 23rd Rajab - 19th May
55	317	Mustafa 'Ali Hudal Reminder of 'Osmān Digna's authority [in context of Hadendawa mutiny] 23rd Rajab - 19th May
57	318	People around Jebel al-Dāyir Order to head for the jebel 23rd Rajab - 19th May
61	319	His beloved and friends, fuqarā' [poor holy men] and the wretched Rare mention of Mahdi's trouble with overwork and his large harem After 23rd Rajab - after 19th May
64	320	'Abdallah Abū-Bakr Strips him of the title of Sultan but urges co-operation with Muhammad Khālid 24th Rajab - 20th May

Volume 3

Page	No.	Recipient – Subject matter – Dates
		1301 – 1884
67	321	Mahmūd ʿAbd-al-Qādir Reply withholding permission to invade lucrative Nuba Mountains 24th Rajab - 20th May
68	322	ʿAbd-al-Samad Sharfi Informs that Ahmad Yāqūb is heading to Dāra to gather his clan 24th Rajab - 20th May
69	323	One of the officials in the Jazīra Reply, giving rulings on various issues Rajab - 27th April-26th May
72	324	Mustafa Yāwir [mudīr (Governor) of Dongola, appointed by Cairo] Refers to earlier appointment as amīr of Dongola region Rajab - 27th April-26th May
75	325	His beloved and followers on the path of Prophet Abolition of titles, e.g. sheikh and sayyid Rajab - 27th April-26th May
77	326	All his beloved Abolition of titles, e.g. sheikh and faqi; amīr to be purely military title Rajab - 27th April-26th May
81	327	His beloved Further note on abolition of titles and status as a way of reducing rivalry Rajab - 27th April-26th May

Volume 3

Page	No.	Recipient – Subject matter – Dates
		1301 – 1884
86	328	Muhammad Sharīf Nūr al-Dā'im Call on former mentor to believe in the Mahdīa Rajab - 27th April-26th May
89	329	Followers of al-Sharīf Ahmad Taha Appointment of Sa'īd Nasr to replace Sharīf Ahmad Taha [see Letter 384] Rajab - 27th April-26th May
90	330	Khalīfa 'Abdullāhi Property of Judge Mirghani to go to his family, not to 'Abd-al-Karīm Kināni Rajab - 27th April-26th May
91	331	Ahmad Suleimān Appointment of Muhammad 'Omar al-Banna and Ahmad al-Nūr as scribes Rajab - 27th April-26th May
93	332	Ahmad 'Omar, Muhammad 'Abd-al-Rahīm and [two named] others Reminder of official duties, under authority of Khalīfa 'Abdullāhi Rajab - 27th April-26th May
96	333	His beloved General call for reliance on God Rajab - 27th April-26th May
100	334	Al-Mak 'Adam 'Omar and others Sending Sheikh Babikr and two deputies to take Jebal Massa loot After Rajab - after 26th May

Volume 3

Page	No.	Recipient – Subject matter - Dates
		1301 – 1884
102	335	Muhammad al-Amīn al-Fulāti Complains that Beit al-Māl is empty and sends 30 riyals After Rajab - after 26th May
103	336	Ahmad Hamza Reply, referring case to Muhammad al-Kheir After Rajab - after 26th May
104	337	al-Hāj al-Sheikh Mahmūd Reply, acknowledging gift and urging obedience to local amīr 4th Shaʿbān - 30th May
106	338	Mahmūd Issa Zāʾid Reply, appointing recipient as amīr but not ʿāmil ʿumūm [senior civilian official] 4th Shaʿbān - 30th May
109	339	All his beloved in God Corporal punishments for men and women shaking hands or embracing 6th Shaʿbān - 1st June
110	340	[From Ahmad ʿAli, Qādi al-Islam] Questions on breast-feeding, menstruation and three other social issues 11th Shaʿbān - 6th June
111	341	Ahmad ʿAli Reply to Letter 340, giving rulings on all five issues under Sharīʿa 11th Shaʿbān - 6th June

Volume 3

Page	No.	Recipient – Subject matter – Dates
		1301 – 1884
114	342	Mahmūd ʿAbd-al-Qādir Requests transport animals 12th Shaʿbān – 7th June
115	343	[From Ahmad al-Nūr] Inquiry about format of Shaʿbān prayers 13th Shaʿbān – 8th June
116	344	Ahmad al-Nūr Reply to Letter 343, clarifying format 14th Shaʿbān – 9th June
117	345	All his beloved Rulings on various issues, including agriculture and land seizure 14th Shaʿbān – 9th June
121	346	ʿAbd-al-Rahmān al-Nujūmi, Hamdān Abū-ʿAnja, etc. Reply, ordering them to return to Jebel Dāyir 18th Shaʿbān – 13th June
122	347	All the faithful, male and female Commentary on Qurʿān verse on aspiration to meet God 20th Shaʿbān – 15th June
124	348	[From Ahmad Suleimān] Complaint about crowds in vicinity of the Beit al-Māl 20th Shaʿbān – 15th June

Volume 3

Page	No.	Recipient – Subject matter - Dates
		1301 – 1884
125	349	Khalīfa ʿAbdullāhi Refers to Letter 348, ordering evacuation of surrounding houses 20th Shaʿbān - 15th June
126	350	Ibrāhīm Mustafa Rulings on wearing gold and ivory, also massage and steam-baths 23rd Shaʿbān - 18th June
128	351	[From Karamallah Sheikh Muhammad] Queries about law, confiscation of property and text of bayʿa [No date]
129	352	Karamallah Sheikh Muhammad Reply to Letter 351, with rulings on return of property and on amputations 23rd Shaʿbān - 18th June
130	353	[From Jīballah Mūsa] Inquiry about purchase of land by Ibrāhīm al-Badawi and resale 24th Shaʿbān - 19th June
131	354	Jīballah Mūsa Reply to Letter 353, clarifying laws on property and land under Mahdīa 24th Shaʿbān - 19th June
132	355	The group of al-Hāj al-Tayyib and surroundings Agrees to Qaili wad al-Ati as amīr under authority of Abū-Sinn clan Shaʿbān - 26th May-24th June

53

Volume 3

Page	No.	Recipient – Subject matter - Dates
		1301 – 1884
134	356	[From ʿAbd-al-Rahmān al-Nujūmi and Hamdān Abū-ʿAnja] Permission to seize foodstuffs and livestock from local population Shaʿbān - 26th May-24th June
135	357	ʿAbd-al-Rahmān al-Nujūmi and Hamdān Abū-ʿAnja Reply to Letter 356, granting authority to seize food and butcher cows Shaʿbān - 26th May-24th June
137	358	Ahmad al-Makāshfi, etc. Urges clan to apply Sharīʿa to their own community as well as others Shaʿbān - 26th May-24th June
140	359	Muhammad Khālid Zughul Explains rank of Mahdi's companions as equal to Prophet's companions Shaʿbān - 26th May-24th June
143	360	Khalīfa ʿAbdullāhi Relays account of ʿAbd-al-Halīm at al-ʿObeid about conditions in Kordofan After Shaʿbān - after 24th June
146	361	His beloved in God Instructions on maintaining the fast correctly 1st Ramadan - 25th June
150	362	Mahmūd ʿAbd-al-Qādir Order to be charitable to the poor and treat local people well 2nd Ramadan - 26th June

54

Volume 3

Page	No.	Recipient – Subject matter – Dates
		1301 – 1884
151	363	Maḥmūd 'Abd-al-Qādir Reply, requesting more arms and ammunition 2nd Ramadan - 26th June
152	364	[From unknown sender] Inquiry about the dowry of a woman divorced before the Mahdīa 2nd or 12th Ramadan - 26th June or 6th July
153	365	[No recipient identified] Reply to Letter 364, clarifying issues of dowry, divorce and repayment 2nd or 12th Ramadan - 26th June or 6th July
154	366	Maḥmūd 'Abd-al-Qādir Orders handover of slave-girl to rightful owner 11th Ramadan - 5th July
155	367	[From Aḥmad Suleimān] Reports that Beit al-Māl is empty; proposes distribution of slaves 11th Ramadan - 5th July
156	368	Aḥmad Suleimān Reply to Letter 367, ordering him to spend what is available After 11th Ramadan - after 5th July
157	369	'Osmān Digna Orders recruitment, not harrassment, of people fleeing from Suakin 18th Ramadan - 12th July

Volume 3

Page	No.	Recipient – Subject matter – Dates
		1301 – 1884
159	370	Muhammad Khālid Zughul Advises recipient to accompany Muhammad al-Kheir Idrīs to the Mahdi 18th Ramadan - 12th July
160	371	The peoples of Suakin Chastises for not joining ʿOsmān Digna but permits them to work as merchants 18th Ramadan - 12th July
163	372	[No recipient identified] Calls for possessions of al-Surra bint al-Naʿma to be returned 19th Ramadan - 13th July
164	373	ʿOsmān Digna Puts confiscation of property on hold pending Mahdi's arrival 20th Ramadan - 14th July
165	374	ʿOsmān Digna Confidence that Khatmīa tarīqa and Shingetti family will be won over 20th Ramadan - 14th July
168	375	al-Hussein ʿAbd-al-Wāhid Reply, informing that aides have been instructed to investigate points raised 20th Ramadan - 14th July
170	376	Muhammad al-Tāhir ibn al-Tayyib Qamr al-Dīn al-Majdhūb Reply, praising him for joining ʿOsmān Digna and mentioning poem from his son 25th Ramadan - 19th July

Volume 3

Page	No.	Recipient – Subject matter - Dates
		1301 – 1884
172	377	Muhammad al-Majdhūb ibn al-Tāhir al-Majdhūb Thanks for poem [see Letter 376] and giving general advice 25th Ramadan - 19th July
174	378	ʿOsmān Digna Condolences on death of Digna's brother ʿOmar in Nuba Mountains campaign 25th Ramadan - 19th July
176	379	al-Amīn Muhammad ʿAli Digna Advice on how to make supplications to God Ramadan - 25th June-24th July
177	380	His beloved, the faithful believers in God, his Book and the Last Day Notes merits of life hereafter, calls for oath of allegiance and urges cohesion Ramadan - 25th June-24th July
181	381	Fakhr al-Dīn Hassan al-Maʿlāwi Condemns recipient's pretence at being a khalīfa [see also Letter 382] 2nd Shawwāl - 26th July
183	382	Fakhr al-Dīn Hassan al-Maʿlāwi Explains real meaning of recipient's dream, in which told he was a khalīfa 4th Shawwāl - 28th July
185	383	Muhammad Khālid Zughul Criticises zakāt officials who intercepted Habbanīa en route to the Mahdi 5th Shawwāl - 29th July

Volume 3

Page	No.	Recipient – Subject matter – Dates
		1301 – 1884
187	384	Muhammad al-Amīn Dafa'allah [and other named recipients] Appointment of Sa'īd Nasr as local amīr under Khalīfa Muhammad Sharīf 5th Shawwāl - 29th July
188	385	Khalīfa 'Abdullāhi Order to release Muhammad Amīn Dafa'allah 5th Shawwāl - 29th July
189	386	The beloved Describes his own "safe passage" in this life and the life hereafter 6th Shawwāl - 30th July
190	387	Mahmūd 'Abd-al-Qādir Stresses importance of Muhammad Musā'id joining the Mahdi 9th Shawwāl - 2nd August
191	388	Karamallah Sheikh Muhammad Calls for advance on Khartoum by river [see Letters 351 and 352] 14th Shawwāl - 7th August
192	389	Followers of the faith with Karamallah Sheikh Muhammad Praise for following Karamallah and urges advance on the capital 14th Shawwāl - 7th August
194	390	Muhammad 'Osmān al-Mīrghani Repeated call to join the movement, preferably under 'Osmān Digna 22nd Shawwāl - 15th August

58

Volume 3

Page	No.	Recipient – Subject matter – Dates
		1301 – 1884
198	391	Muḥammad Khālid Zughul Order to return looted property to Misairīa and Fallāta and stop violations 24th Shawwāl - 17th August
200	392	To the sheikhs and people south of Eastern Sudan [i.e. in Eritrea] Appointment of al-Hussein 'Ali as local amīr 25th Shawwāl - 18th August
202	393	Maḥmūd 'Abd-al-Qādir Order to send Abābda tribesmen and French national [Olivier Pain] 28th Shawwāl - 21st August
203	394	al-Hussein 'Abd-al-Wāhid, etc. Maḥmūd Issa, Saleh and 'Abdallah Abū-Sinn as leaders under al-Hussein 29th Shawwāl - 22nd August
206	395	Muḥammad Khālid Zughul Rebuke for detaining would-be migrants and stealing their property Shawwāl - 25th July-22nd Aug
208	396	Sons of Nūr al-Dā'im Reply to complaint about harsh letter from Khalīfa 'Abdullāhi Shawwāl - 25th July-22nd Aug
211	397	Gordon Pasha Call for surrender and conversion to Islam Shawwāl - 25th July-22nd Aug

Volume 3

Page	No.	Recipient – Subject matter – Dates
		1301 – 1884
218	398	The people of Dār Umūma [Kordofan] Permits women to remain to manage farms while men rally to Khartoum 1st Dhū al-Qaʿda – 23rd August
221	399	ʿAbd-al-Samad Sharfi Reply to earlier letters, one of them about al-Tāhir al-Tijāni 7th Dhū al-Qaʿda – 29th August
222	400	Mahmūd ʿAbd-al-Qādir Acknowledges arrival of al-Haran al-Bashīr, Olivier Pain and four Abābda 12th Dhū al-Qaʿda – 3rd September
223	401	Mahmūd ʿAbd-al-Qādir Reply, announcing pardon for all muhājirīn [people who migrate to join Mahdīa] 14th Dhū al-Qaʿda – 5th September
224	402	Ahmad ʿAli, the Qādi al-Islam Request to investigate complaint by a woman about a murder 14th Dhū al-Qaʿda – 5th September
225	403	[From Muhammad al-Kheir ʿAbdallah Khojali] Request for guidance on land ownership, taxation and marriage contracts 1st Ramadan – 24th July
227	404	Muhammad al-Kheir ʿAbdallah Khojali Reply to Letter 403, giving rulings on land issues and dowry donations 16th Dhū al-Qaʿda – 7th September

Volume 3

Page	No.	Recipient – Subject matter – Dates
		1301 – 1884
229	405	The people of Rufaʿa [on the Blue Nile] Reply, praising them and asking them to join siege of Khartoum 17th Dhū al-Qaʿda - 8th September
231	406	ʿAbd-al-Samad Sharfi Asks recipient and Muhammad Khālid to join him in advance on Khartoum 18th Dhū al-Qaʿda - 9th September
232	407	The mulāzimīn [religious police] Warning not to be heavy-handed and vulgar with the faithful 26th Dhū al-Qaʿda - 17th September
234	408	Muhammad Khālid Zughul Reports arrival and pardon of al-Tāhir al-Tijāni, orders return of property Dhū al-Qaʿda - 23rd Aug-21st Sept
235	409	His beloved in God Long lecture on morality, jihād and the promise of victory 8th Dhū al-Hijja - 29th September
244	410	Muhammad Khālid Zughul Informs about betrayal of Mustafa Yāwir, Mudīr of Dongola 8th Dhū al-Hijja - 29th September
246	411	Ahmad Jamāl al-Dīn and Muhammad Nūr Mahmūd ʿAbd-al-Rahman Condolences for death of uncle Mahmūd al-Hāj Muhammad 8th Dhū al-Hijja - 29th September

Volume 3

Page	No.	Recipient – Subject matter - Dates
		1301 – 1884
247	412	Ahmad Jamāl al-Dīn and Muhammad Nūr Mahmūd ʿAbd-al-Rahman [Copy of Letter 411] 8th Dhū al-Hijja - 29th September
248	413	Ahmad Jamāl al-Dīn and relatives of Mahmūd the martyr Urging recipients to make the hijra and join advance on Khartoum 8th Dhū al-Hijja - 29th September
251	414	His beloved in God General moral pep-talk on consequences of evading jihād 13th Dhū al-Hijja - 5th October
253	415	ʿAbd-al-Samad Sharfi Refers to earlier message [Letter 406] and repeats call to come separately 13th Dhū al-Hijja - 5th October
254	416	Muhammad al-Faqi Ahmad [at Atbara] and those with him Thanks for joining siege of Khartoum and call for reinforcements 14th Dhū al-Hijja - 6th October
256	417	Mahmūd ʿAbd-al-Qādir Gives details of siege, calls for Karkasāwi to come from Bahr al-Ghazāl 17th Dhū al-Hijja - 9th October

Volume 3

Page	No.	Recipient – Subject matter – Dates
		1301 – 1884
258	418	His beloved faithful Very long sermon on moral issues, stoicism and priority of hijra and jihād Before 19th Dhū al-Hijja - before 10th October
273	419	[A sermon on the meaning of the first sūra of the Qur'ān] Religious sermon on mercy in the afterlife and Allah's judgement Before 19th Dhū al-Hijja - before 10th October
276	420	His companions and his beloved Long sermon on enduring hard times and obeying umarā' and khulafā' 19th Dhū al-Hijja - 10th October
289	421	The people of Khartoum Criticism for reliance on the English, urges surrender and promises safety After 20th Dhū al-Hijja - after 12th October
291	422	Muhammad Khālid Zughul Mahmūd 'Abd-al-Qādir to go to Dongola, 'Abd-al-Samad Sharfi to Kordofan 21st Dhū al-Hijja - 13th October
292	423	'Abd-al-Samad Sharfi Variation on Letter 422, ordering immediate move to al-'Obeid 21st Dhū al-Hijja - 13th October
293	424	Mahmūd 'Abd-al-Qādir Variation on Letter 422, noting also 'Abd-al-Halīm Musā'id going to al-'Obeid 21st Dhū al-Hijja - 13th October

Volume 3

Page	No.	Recipient – Subject matter – Dates
		1301 – 1884
295	425	Khalīfa ʿAbdullāhi Consultation on various appointments 21st Dhū al-Hijja - 13th October
296	426	Mīrghani Suwār al-Dahab Reply, requesting doctors to treat those suffering from smallpox After 26th Dhū al-Hijja - after 18th October
297	427	al-Nujūmi, ʿAbdallah al-Nūr and Abū-Girja Scolding for complaints against al-Basīr family for not delivering sorghum Dhū al-Hijja - 22nd Sept-20th Oct
305	428	[From ʿAbdallah Abbūd] Seeking accreditation as amīr, having secured consent of Muhammad wad al-Basīr Dhū al-Hijja - 22nd Sept-20th Oct
306	429	ʿAbdallah Abūd Reply to Letter 428, informing that al-Daw wad al-Tayyib appointed Dhū al-Hijja - 22nd Sept-20th Oct
307	430	Hamid al-Nīl Hāmid Instructions on caring for his followers with kindness and charity [During 1301] - 2nd Nov 1883-20th Oct 1884
309	431	The beloved Scornful query as to why they have not joined the jihād [During 1301] - 2nd Nov 1883-20th Oct 1884

Volume 3

Page	No.	Recipient – Subject matter - Dates
		1301 – 1883-4
312	432	His beloved and companions Ordeals are a test from God, calls for stoicism [During 1301] - 2nd Nov 1883-20th Oct 1884
314	433	Idrīs al-Sāyir Instruction to treat prisoners well, only to whip them on qāḍi's orders [During 1301] - 2nd Nov 1883-20th Oct 1884
315	434	ʿAbdallah Jubāra Request to settle camel-hire tariff with Governor of the Beit al-Māl [During 1301] - 2nd Nov 1883-20th Oct 1884
317	435	Ahmad ibn al-Amīn Reply about complaint about not being appointed amīr [During 1301] - 2nd Nov 1883-20th Oct 1884
318	436	Khalīfa ʿAbdullāhi Commuting death sentences to amputations and 80 lashes [During 1301] - 2nd Nov 1883-20th Oct 1884
319	437	al-faqi Muhammad al-Amīn, al-faqi Hamīd, etc. Notice that all sects and Sufi turuq [brotherhoods] have been abolished [During 1301] - 2nd Nov 1883-20th Oct 1884
321	438	Khalīfa ʿAbdullāhi Order to incorporate al-Sharīf Hamad al-Nīl's men under the Black Flag [During 1301] - 2nd Nov 1883-20th Oct 1884

Volume 3

Page	No.	Recipient – Subject matter - Dates
		1301 – 1883-4
322	439	People of the river territories [Upper Egypt] Information about the Mahdīa, condemnation of tyrants of Egypt [During 1301] - 2nd Nov 1883-20th Oct 1884
326	440	His beloved, the believers in the Book and the Sunna Informs that he is sending men to support them in attacks on Turks [During 1301] - 2nd Nov 1883-20th Oct 1884
328	441	Ahmad Suleimān Money from Beit al-Māl for poor mujāhidīn only [During 1301] - 2nd Nov 1883-20th Oct 1884
330	442	al-Mudathir Ibrāhīm, his beloved Reminder that God evaluates deeds in accordance with intentions [During 1301] - 2nd Nov 1883-20th Oct 1884
333	443	The beloved, those who have made hijra and supporters of jihād Explains revered status of Mahdi's earliest supporters [During 1301] - 2nd Nov 1883-20th Oct 1884
337	444	His beloved in God Call for recipients to migrate to the Mahdi and pledge allegiance [During 1301] - 2nd Nov 1883-20th Oct 1884
341	445	Muhammad Ahmad Umm Bireir Reply, advising that requested money is on its way but scorning materialism [During 1301] - 2nd Nov 1883-20th Oct 1884

Volume 3

Page	No.	Recipient – Subject matter – Dates
		1301 – 1883-4
343	446	Khalīfa 'Abdullāhi Order to release prisoner 'Abdullāhi al-Khalīfa and hand over to him [see Letter 448] [During 1301] - 2nd Nov 1883-20th Oct 1884
345	447	Khalīfa 'Abdullāhi [Copy of Letter 446] [During 1301] - 2nd Nov 1883-20th Oct 1884
346	448	'Abdullāhi al-Khalīfa States that imprisonment was beneficial, improve behaviour in future [During 1301] - 2nd Nov 1883-20th Oct 1884
348	449	'Attā al-Manān al-Suleihābi Orders people of Rufā'a to collaborate with Jānqī [southerners] [During 1301] - 2nd Nov 1883-20th Oct 1884
350	450	Mahmūd 'Abd-al-Qādir Help 'Abdallah Jubāra and Fallāta transport families from Nuba Mountains [During 1301] - 2nd Nov 1883-20th Oct 1884
351	451	[From Ahmad al-Nūr] Request for advice [During 1301] - 2nd Nov 1883-20th Oct 1884
352	452	Ahmad al-Nūr Reply to Letter 451, authorising despatch of the "Hudūd Edict" [During 1301] - 2nd Nov 1883-20th Oct 1884

Volume 4

Vol 4		274 letters (20th October 1884 - 16th May 1885)
Page	No.	Recipient – Subject matter - Dates

1302 - 1884

1	453	His beloved and companions Urges followers not to be competitive about living close to Mahdi 1st Muharram - 21st October
3	454	Muhammad al-Kheir 'Abdallah Khojali Order of seizure of loot from Berber and allocation to Beit al-Māl 1st Muharram - 21st October
8	455	Gordon Pasha Informs of death of Europeans [on the steamer 'Abbās], gloats over captured mail 2nd Muharram - 22nd October
14	456	[From Ahmad Suleimān] Request for advice on marriage, given already married to four women 3rd Muharram - 23rd October
15	457	Ahmad Suleimān Reply to Letter 456, agreeing to marriage if one earlier wife divorced 3rd Muharram - 23rd October
16	458	'Abdallah Awad al-Karīm Abū-Sinn Appointment as amīr of Rufā'a, under Nujūmi and Abū-Girja 5th Muharram - 25th October

Volume 4

Page	No.	Recipient – Subject matter - Dates
		1302 - 1884
19	459	Ahmad al-Tayyib al-Basīr Appointment as amīr of Halawiyīn, outlining limits of authority 6th or 9th Muharram - 26th or 29th October
21	460	'Abd-al-Rahmān al-Qurāshi Notice of above appointment [Letter 459] and demand for co-operation 6th or 9th Muharram - 26th or 29th October
23	461	Muhammad Abū-Hijil and his Rubātab Praise for killing Europeans [on the 'Abbās], follow orders of Muhammad al-Kheir 10th Muharram - 30th October
25	462	Mahmūd 'Abd-al-Qādir Refers to ammunition sent and letter sent to Gordon [Letter 455] 10th Muharram - 30th October
27	463	'Abd-al-Samad Sharfi Comment on mutiny of Daūd Binjah, notice of arrival at al-Fiteihāb 10th Muharram - 30th October
29	464	Ahmad al-Tayyib al-Basīr Repeats news of appointment as amīr of Halawiyīn, under Nujūmi and Abū-Girja 12th Muharram - 1st November
32	465	Sālih al-Mak Refers to hypocrisy in Sālih's letter to Gordon, promises imprisonment not death 14th Muharram - 3rd November

Volume 4

Page	No.	Recipient – Subject matter - Dates
		1302 - 1884
34	466	Sālih al-Mak States that imprisonment is for reform not punishment 14th Muharram - 3rd November
35	467	Sālih al-Mak States that imprisonment is for reform not revenge After 14th Muharram - after 3rd November
37	468	'Abdallah al-Muslimāni [Frank Lupton, in Equatoria] Anger at Lupton's hypocrisy in letter to Gordon claiming conversion was coerced 20th Muharram - 9th November
39	469	[From 'Abdallah al-Nūr] Account of dream in which strong wind carries off all but the Mahdi 28th Muharram - 18th November
41	470	'Abdallah al-Nūr Reply to Letter 469, commenting that dream illustrates virtues of poverty and jihād 28th Muharram - 18th November
43	471	His beloved and his intimate elite [Amended copy of Letter 470] 28th Muharram - 18th November
45	472	Gordon Pasha Informs of arrival near Omdurman; English at Dongola will share Hicks' fate 29th Muharram - 19th November

70

Volume 4

Page	No.	Recipient – Subject matter – Dates
		1302 - 1884
46	473	Officers of Omdurman Post Refers to former relationship with Farajallah [Rāghib], reiterates battles won End of Muharram - 19th November
48	474	The peoples of the Halawiyīn and residents of [Wad] Medani Appointment of Ahmad al-Tayyib al-Basīr [see Letters 459 and 464] Muharram - 21st Oct-19th Nov
51	475	[Various named tribes of Gedaref] Call to accept leadership of 'Abdallah Ahmad Abū-Sinn, urges payment of zakāt 1st Safar - 20th November
54	476	All companions, followers, umarā', brigade commanders and muqaddamīn Registration of all troops on pay-lists, all loot to Beit al-Māl 1st Safar - 20th November
55	477	Muhammad al-Kheir 'Abdallah Khojali Supplement [to Letter 404] on issues of land and property ownership 3rd Safar - 22nd November
57	478	Muhammad al-Kheir 'Abdallah Khojali Order that all umarā' with loot from Berber must take to Beit al-Māl 3rd Safar - 22nd November

Volume 4

Page	No.	Recipient – Subject matter – Dates
		1302 – 1884
66	479	His beloved and intimate among the Anṣār of the Faith [Amended copy of Letter 471] 3rd Safar – 22nd November
73	480	Muhammad al-Kheir 'Abdallah Khojali Refers to incidents at al-'Obeid to illustrate dangers of scramble for loot 3rd Safar – 22nd November
79	481	'Abdallah al-Nūr Requests copy of Letter 480 for correction and re-sending to Berber 3rd Safar – 22nd November
80	482	Muhammad Suleimān Refers to error in Letter 480, requesting correction and re-sending 3rd Safar – 22nd November
81	483	Khashm al-Mūs Bīk and those with him [Copy of Letter 473, without personal introduction] 5th Safar – 24th November
83	484	Khalīfa 'Abdullāhi States that Letter 473 has not arrived, requests copy addressed to Nusshi Pasha 5th Safar – 24th November
84	485	All his beloved at Berber Ruling on possessions of al-Sawārāb, al-Hankāb and al-'Awnīa tribes 7th Safar – 26th November

Volume 4

Page	No.	Recipient – Subject matter - Dates
		1302 - 1884
85	486	'Abd-al-Rahmān al-Nujūmi and 'Abdallah al-Nūr Moralistic lecture on bearing up at difficult times 10th Safar - 29th November
94	487	His beloved and intimate among the Ansār of the Faith [Amended copy of Letter 486] 10th Safar - 29th November
107	488	Supporters in the markets Rules on currency equivalents and exchange rates [European and regional] 12th Safar - 1st December
108	489	The Ja'aliyīn of Gedaref Explains percentages for zakāt, notes on punishments and ban of popular games 25th Safar - 14th December
110	490	Muhammad al-Taweim the Praise-Singer Reply, praising him and his work 25th Safar - 14th December
111	491	Hamid al-Nīl Hāmid Reply to request, explaining that ordeals should be faced with endurance and prayers 25th Safar - 14th December
113	492	[From Ahmad Suleimān] Details 4,699 Khartoum residents who have fled, to be supported by Beit al-Māl 26th Safar - 15th December

Volume 4

Page	No.	Recipient – Subject matter - Dates
		1302 - 1884
115	493	Ahmad Suleimān Reply to Letter 492, urging treatment of refugees with compassion 26th Safar - 15th December
116	494	ʿAbdallah Muhammad Jubāra Denies authorship of leaflet banning prayers for souls of those who had not made the hjira 28th Safar - 17th December
117	495	Ahmad Muhammad Abū-Sharīʿa Permission to sing in praise of the Prophet, the Mahdi and jihād 29th Safar - 18th December
118	496	[From Ahmad Suleimān] Reply to inquiry about personal expenditure, describes selling camels in lieu of gold Safar - 20th Nov-18th Dec
120	497	Ahmad Suleimān Reply to Letter 496, praising recipient for settling personal debts 26th Safar - 15th December
121	498	ʿAbdallah Ahmad Abū-Sinn Discussion of request for local amīr, order to appoint one of two candidates 1st Rabīʿ I - 19th December
122	499	His deputies and Ansār in the Jazīra Informs that sons of al-Bashīr Nūr al-Dāʾim permitted to join siege of Sennār 2nd Rabīʿ I - 20th December

Volume 4

Page	No.	Recipient – Subject matter - Dates
		1302 - 1884
123	500	His deputies and Ansār in Kāmlīn Permission granted to al-Tayyib Nūr al-Dā'im to exploit land of Ahmad Pasha 2nd Rabī' I - 20th December
124	501	Muhammad Sālih Sāti Refers to arrival from Dongola and assuages anxiety about family left there 2nd Rabī' I - 20th December
128	502	His beloved and aides in Metemma and Shendi [north of Khartoum] Praise for sinking one government steamer and hitting another, as reported by Sa'ad Farah 3rd Rabī' I - 21st December
130	503	Muhammad al-Kheir 'Abdallah Khojali Refers to correspondence between recipient and Salih Hussein Khalīfa 3rd Rabī' I - 21st December
131	504	Muhammad Abū-Hijil Reply, instructing him to remain where he is and exert himself in the jihād 3rd Rabī' I - 21st December
132	505	Inhabitants of Tayyiba Approves merger with 'Abd-al-Rahmān al-Qurāshi 3rd Rabī' I - 21st December
133	506	Mustafa 'Ali Hadal Notice of appointment of Muhammad Ibrāhīm Dāwi as amīr over the Humrān 4th Rabī' I - 22nd December

Volume 4

Page	No.	Recipient – Subject matter – Dates
		1302 – 1884
134	507	Muhammad Ibrāhīm Dhāwi Notice of appointment as amīr over the Humrān, under ʿOsmān Digna's leadership 4th Rabīʿ I – 22nd December
135	508	Mahmūd ʿAbd-al-Qādir Requests more diligence in procuring and sending on ammunition from Darfur 4th Rabīʿ I – 22nd December
136	509	His beloved in God Commentary on stoicism and faith in times of need and loss of livelihood 5th Rabīʿ I – 23rd December
140	510	Awad al-Karīm al-Kāfūt Appointment of Muhammad Ibrāhīm Dāwi [see Letters 506 and 507], noting personal friendship 6th Rabīʿ I – 24th December
141	511	ʿAbdallah ibn Abū-Bakr Reply to complaint about killings by Muhammad Khālid Zughul; inquiry to be intitiated 7th Rabīʿ I – 25th December
144	512	ʿAbd-al-Halīm Musāʿid Refers to complaint by ʿOsmān Sālih Arbāwi, ordering return of detainees and their property 7th Rabīʿ I – 25th December
146	513	Al-Tāhir Muhammad Tātāi Criticism of dispute between recipient, al-Hussein ʿAbd-al-Wāhid and al-Samni Ahmad 7th Rabīʿ I – 25th December

Volume 4

Page	No.	Recipient – Subject matter - Dates
		1302 - 1884
148	514	al-Hussein ʿAbd-al-Wāhid Nūr al-Dāʿim Ruling that dispute [see Letter 513] is an error on all sides 7th Rabīʿ I - 25th December
150	515	Muhammad Khālid Zughul Refers to complainants, ordering their release and return of confiscated possessions 7th Rabīʿ I - 25th December
151	516	ʿAbd-al-Rahmān al-Nujūmi Approves tactics mentioned in letter to Khalīfa, ordering deployment to Bari to await attack 8th Rabīʿ I - 26th December
154	517	ʿAbd-al-Rahmān al-Nujūmi Those caught harbouring the messengers of the infidels to be released if innocence proven 9th Rabīʿ I - 27th December
155	518	Gordon Pasha Reiterates call to surrender and be pardoned, pledges to wipe out Relief Expedition 9th Rabīʿ I - 27th December
157	519	Those entering Khartoum and those already there Warning against hoarding loot, which should all be handed to Beit al-Māl 10th Rabīʿ I - 28th December
159	520	ʿAbdallah Ahmad Abū-Sinn Requests recipient and others to appoint an overall amīr 11th Rabīʿ I - 29th December

Volume 4

Page	No.	Recipient – Subject matter – Dates
		1302 – 1884
160	521	Fadl al-Karīm al-Sharīf Praise for abandoning Khartoum, orders to join the forces of al-Mardi Abū-Rof 11th Rabīʿ I – 29th December
161	522	The Anṣār heading to al-Sabalūqa [Gorge, north of Khartoum] Order to obey named umarāʾ and not interfere with local population or property 12th Rabīʿ I – 30th December
162	523	ʿAbd-al-Ḥalīm Musāʿid Asks for lists to clarify legitimate loot, denies recipient right to choose zakāt collectors 12th Rabīʿ I – 30th December
164	524	al-Tayyib Ahmad Hāshim Praises his poem 12th Rabīʿ I – 30th December
165	525	Muhammad al-Kheir ʿAbdallah Khojali Reply, noting receipt of letter from those besieging Shendi and Metemma 12th Rabīʿ I – 30th December
167	526	Ahmad Hāshim Reply, referring to old friendship 12th Rabīʿ I – 30th December
168	527	Muhammad al-Kheir ʿAbdallah Khojali Comment on hijra of recipient's wife and brother 12th Rabīʿ I – 30th December

Volume 4

Page	No.	Recipient – Subject matter - Dates
		1302 - 1884
169	528	Muhammad Tāhir ʿAbdallah Appointment of recipient's son ʿAbdallah as local amīr, urges support and acceptance 12th Rabīʿ I - 30th December
170	529	Saʿad Ahmad Badr Confirms decree of Khalīfa ʿAbdullāhi on following former sheikhs if they join Mahdīa 12th Rabīʿ I - 30th December
171	530	al-ʿAtta Muhammad al-Dawūd Appointment as amīr of the Sarawrāb, orders deployment to Deim al-Sharq 12th Rabīʿ I - 30th December
173	531	Ahmad Muhammad Kheir Instruction to head for al-Sabalūqa with Ahmad Mustafa 12th Rabīʿ I - 30th December
174	532	Ahmad Suleimān Permission to marry 12th Rabīʿ I - 30th December
175	533	Mahmūd ʿAbd-al-Qādir Describes siege of Khartoum and surrender of Omdurman garrison 12th Rabīʿ I - 30th December
178	534	ʿAli Marhūm Refers to the Hayāt al-Dīn proclamation for guidance on debts and claiming repayment 12th Rabīʿ I - 30th December

Volume 4

Page	No.	Recipient – Subject matter – Dates
		1302 – 1885
182	535	Sālih Hussein Khalīfa Noting virtues of Muhammad al-Kheir and his father, says Relief Expedition is doomed 13th Rabī' I – 1st January
184	536	Muhammad Khālid Zughul Stresses compassion, refers to complaint by Fallāta against over-zealous zakāt collectors 14th Rabī' I – 2nd January
186	537	All his companions Those who cannot attend communal prayers, e.g. the sick, may pray alone 15th Rabī' I – 3rd January
187	538	His beloved and companions Compulsory reading of the Rātib mornings and evenings 15th Rabī' I – 3rd January
189	539	The beloved Determination to punish those who reject the Mahdīa in the capital after conquest of provinces 15th Rabī' I – 3rd January
190	540	Hamid al-Nīl Hāmid Prohibition on selling the wife of Farajallah al-Zeini 17th Rabī' I – 5th January
191	541	al-Majdhūb Abū-Bakr Yūsuf Request to give poet Muhammad al-Tawayyim copy of proclamation on capture of Khartoum 18th Rabī' I – 6th January

Volume 4

Page	No.	Recipient – Subject matter – Dates
		1302 – 1885
192	542	[No recipient identified] Rulings on issues of divorce and polygamy 18th Rabīʿ I – 6th January
197	543	Khalīfa ʿAbdullāhi Only government property to be confiscated from surrendered Omdurman garrison 18th Rabīʿ I – 6th January
198	544	His beloved and intimate Ansār besieging Khartoum Urges humane treatment of refugees from Khartoum, respect for figures like [al-Amīn] al-Darīr 19th Rabīʿ I – 7th January
201	545	Gordon Pasha Forgives Gordon's refusal to surrender but repeats urging to embrace Islam 20th Rabīʿ I – 8th January
203	546	Mahmūd ʿAbd-al-Qādir Orders deployment to meet British relief force near Metemma, resign Dongola position 21st Rabīʿ I – 9th January
204	547	al-Hussein ʿAbd-al-Wāhid Nūr al-Dāʿim More on dispute [see Letters 513 and 514] urging swift resolution 22nd Rabīʿ I – 10th January

Volume 4

Page	No.	Recipient – Subject matter – Dates
		1302 - 1885
205	548	His beloved in God, the people of al-Massallamīa [on the Blue Nile] Appointment of legal expert to settle Sharī'a disputes 23rd Rabī' I - 11th January
206	549	Khalīfa 'Abdullāhi Postpones Ahmad al-Mikāshfi expedition against the British, details of alternative commanders 23rd Rabī' I - 11th January
207	550	Gordon Pasha Offers safe transfer to relief force on surrender; warns fall of Khartoum is imminent 25th Rabī' I - 13th January
209	551	'Osmān Digna Update on surrender of Omfurman fort, deserters from Khartoum and imminent fall of city 26th Rabī' I - 14th January
212	552	Ahmad ibn al-Hāj Abi al-Majdhūb Permission to open Qur'ān school on condition he joins jihād when summoned 27th Rabī' I - 15th January
213	553	'Abdallah ibn Muhammad [Copy of Letter 552] [No date]
214	554	His beloved officials and deputies Permission granted to Muhammad Beni Rāghib to bring his family 27th Rabī' I - 15th January

Volume 4

Page	No.	Recipient – Subject matter – Dates
		1302 - 1885
215	555	Mahmūd 'Issa Zā'id Incorporation into his ranks of some Ansār who complained about their former commander 27th Rabī' I - 15th January
216	556	All his beloved in God Illustrates how incantations may be recited and when Before 28th Rabī' I - before 16th January
217	557	Ahmad Jamāl al-Dīn, Muhammad Nūr Mahmūd, etc. Scorn for their not following the Mahdīa and urging to do so quickly 28th Rabī' I - 16th January
218	558	[From Ahmad al-Nūr] Following instruction on incantations, requests advice on asking blessings for the Prophet 28th Rabī' I - 16th January
219	559	Ahmad al-Nūr Reply to Letter 558, providing instruction on asking for God's forgiveness 28th Rabī' I - 16th January
220	560	'Osmān Digna Appointment of Muhammad 'Ali Kartūb and Muhammad al-Faqih Hamad over the Shukrīa End of Rabī' I - 18th January
221	561	The Halāwiyīn on the River Atbara Appointment of Muhammad al-Faqih Hamad as their amīr End of Rabī' I - 18th January

Volume 4

Page	No.	Recipient – Subject matter – Dates
		1302 – 1885
222	562	Fātima, daughter of Hārūn Condolences on death of husband; free choice on re-marriage 2nd Rabīʿ II – 20th January
223	563	Sayyidein Yūnus al-Burdanein Notes wish of Ibrāhīm ʿAmūri to join Mahdīa, urges recipients to leave Khartoum and be forgiven 3rd Rabīʿ II – 21st January
225	564	Zarūq al-Tāhir, etc. [Copy of Letter 563] 3rd Rabīʿ II – 21st January
226	565	Ibrāhīm Abū-ʿAmūri Offers safe passage and pardon in return for swift departure from Khartoum [No date]
227	566	Muhammad Khālid Zughul Refers to bond between recipient and Mahmūd ʿAbd-al-Qādir, also gossip of Muhammad Kheir Baʿdi 5th Rabīʿ II – 23rd January
230	567	Omar Muhammad Kheir Terhu Reply referring to gossip of Muhammad Kheir Baʿdi, urges continuation of assistance to Muhammad Khālid 5th Rabīʿ II – 23rd January

Volume 4

Page	No.	Recipient – Subject matter - Dates
		1302 - 1885
231	568	Muhammad Suleimān Approves draft of above [Letters 566 and 567], requesting fair copy for addition of footnote 5th Rabīʿ II - 23rd January
232	569	ʿAbdallah Ahmad Abū-Sinn Appointment as amīr of Atbara River district, authority to appoint subordinates 5th Rabīʿ II - 23rd January
233	570	Ahmad al-Nūr Reply, requesting someone to be sent to comfort recipient's mother 5th Rabīʿ II - 23rd January
234	571	al-Nūr Muhammad Angara Noting contents of letter from Abū-Safīya, thanks and pledges to send army as requested [During 1302] - 21st Oct 1884-10th Oct 1885
236	572	Muhammad ʿOsmān Abū-Girja Declines request to resign, instead appointing to lead forces sent against British 6th Rabīʿ II - 24th January
238	573	Khalīfa ʿAbdullāhi Order to settle dispute between Abū-Garja and other commanders in Khartoum district 6th Rabīʿ II - 24th January
240	574	[From ʿAbdallah al-Tayyib Qamr al-Dīn al-Majdhūb] Inquiring about use of singular or plural in Rātib 7th Rabīʿ II - 25th January

Volume 4

Page	No.	Recipient – Subject matter – Dates
		1302 – 1885
241	575	'Abdallah al-Tayyib Qamr al-Dīn al-Majdhūb Reply to Letter 574, with explanation 7th Rabī' II – 25th January
242	576	Gordon Pasha Reminder of previous warnings and warning that nothing can be expected from Relief Expedition Before 9th Rabī' II – before 27th January
245	577	Khalīfa 'Abdullāhi Advice that all commanders watch out for their property at fall of Khartoum Before 9th Rabī' II – before 27th January
246	578	Shukrīa living in Atbara River district Appointment of Muhammad 'Ali Kartūb as amīr [see Letter 560], call to advance on Khartoum 9th Rabī' II – 27th January
247	579	Followers of al-'Ubeid Badr Condolences on death of al-'Ubeid Badr, appointment of his son as amīr After 9th Rabī' II – after 27th January
250	580	Ahmad Suleimān Order to support families of al-'Ubeid Badr and Hussein Khalīfa with suitable sums 9th Rabī' II – 27th January
251	581	Bilāl Ramadhān Regrets attack by Muhammad 'Osmān, suggesting mitigating circumstances After 9th Rabī' II – after 27th January

Volume 4

Page	No.	Recipient – Subject matter - Dates
		1302 - 1885
252	582	Khalīfa Sharīf Orders eviction of followers from house of Beit al-Māl servant Asta Bilāl 9th Rabīʿ II - 27th January
253	583	Ahmad Muhammad Hāj Sharīf Assignment in charge of Beit al-Māl's fruit/date orchards After 9th Rabīʿ II - after 27th January
255	584	Khalīfa ʿAbdullāhi Notice on duty to bury the dead, even the infidels of Khartoum After 9th Rabīʿ II - after 27th January
256	585	[From the three khulafāʾ] Still awaiting a boat to cross to Khartoum After 9th Rabīʿ II - after 27th January
257	586	The three khulafāʾ Reply to Letter 585, ordering them to cross without delay by any means necessary After 9th Rabīʿ II - after 27th January
258	587	Ahmad Suleimān Stresses importance of firearms After 9th Rabīʿ II - after 27th January
259	588	Ahmad Suleimān Orders humane treatment for the womenfolk of Khartoum's dignitaries After 9th Rabīʿ II - after 27th January

Volume 4

Page	No.	Recipient – Subject matter - Dates
		1302 - 1885
260	589	Those leaving Khartoum Asks for honest declaration and listing of property After 9th Rabīʻ II - after 27th January
262	590	Bābikr ʻAmr Request for Ansār to treat senior clerics of Khartoum well, especially Muhammad al-Amīn al-Darīr After 9th Rabīʻ II - after 27th January
263	591	Khalīfa ʻAbdullāhi Example of Sheikh Mūsa, allowed to keep property, not to be judged on his past After 9th Rabīʻ II - after 27th January
264	592	Khalīfa ʻAbdullāhi and Khalīfa ʻAli al-Helu Attack by Muhammad Karīb and others on amīn of Beit al-Māl; order to jail them at al-Sāyir After 9th Rabīʻ II - after 27th January
265	593	Telegraph operators Urges them to read the Rātib and perform their work for God After 9th Rabīʻ II - after 27th January
267	594	Mahmūd ʻAbd-al-Qādir Request to facilitate migration of Ansār families to al-Buqʻa [Omdurman] After 9th Rabīʻ II - after 27th January

Volume 4

Page	No.	Recipient – Subject matter - Dates
		1302 - 1885
268	595	Mustafa ʿAli Hadal Shukrīa complaints about raids by ʿAwad al-Karīm al-Kāfūt, orders investigation and return of property 12th Rabīʿ II - 30th January
270	596	Mustafa ʿAli Hadal Notifies him of the fall of Khartoum 12th Rabīʿ II - 30th January
271	597	Mahmūd ʿAbd-al-Qādir Notifies him of the fall of Khartoum 12th Rabīʿ II - 30th January
273	598	[From Muhammad ʿOsmān Abū-Girja Request by Khartoum escapees to return to wives, question about new marriage contracts 12th or 21st Rabīʿ I - 31st Dec 1884 or 9th Jan 1885
274	599	Muhammad ʿOsmān Abū-Girja Reply to Letter 598, confirming necessity of new marriage contracts 12th or 21st Rabīʿ I - 31st Dec 1884 or 9th Jan 1885
275	600	[From Ahmad Suleimān] Discussion of preparations by Abū-Girja and [al-Sheikh] Fādhlu Ahmad for expedition to the north 12th Rabīʿ II - 30th January
277	601	Ahmad Suleimān Reply to Letter 600, informing that Mahdi will perform Friday prayers in Khartoum, streets to be cleaned 14th Rabīʿ II - 1st February

Volume 4

Page	No.	Recipient – Subject matter – Dates
		1302 - 1885
278	602	Maḥmūd Issa Zā'id Notifies him of the fall of Khartoum 14th Rabī' II - 1st February
280	603	Muḥammad Khālid Zughul Notifies him of the fall of Khartoum 14th Rabī' II - 1st February
281	604	'Abdallah Aḥmad Abū-Sinn Notifies him of the fall of Khartoum [No date]
282	605	al-Ṭāhir Muḥammad Tātāi Notifies him of the fall of Khartoum 14th Rabī' II - 1st February
284	606	Khalīfa 'Abdullāhi Divides the Jihādīa among the umarā', orders Khalīfa al-Sharīf division to give belongings to al-Nujūmi 17th Rabī' II - 4th February
285	607	Children of al-Sheikh Idris walad al-Arbāb Chooses 'Ali Hamad Barakāt to succeed his father as clan leader 17th Rabī' II - 4th February
286	608	His officials, deputies and Anṣār Ban on marriage between Anṣār and women leaving Khartoum, unmarried women to Beit al-Māl 18th Rabī' II - 5th February

Volume 4

Page	No.	Recipient – Subject matter – Dates
		1302 - 1885
288	609	[No recipient identified] Refers to death of recipient's brother, alludes to praise of recipient by ʿAbd-al-Qādir Ahmad 18th Rabīʿ II - 5th February
289	610	al-Sheikh Fadhlu Ahmad Clarification of rules on treatment of those leaving Khartoum, including dowries After 18th Rabīʿ II - after 5th February
290	611	The amnāʾ [bureaucrats] Order to return a wife to her husband and scorn man who snatched her After 18th Rabīʿ II - after 5th February
291	612	His beloved the Ansār of the faith Ignore loot, be sincere about jihād, be patient until all loot collected and English defeated 19th Rabīʿ II - 6th February
293	613	Muhammad Abū-Hijil Reply, ordering recipient to follow Muhammad al-Kheir 22nd Rabīʿ II - 9th February
294	614	[From Ahmad Suleimān] Insists on detailed accounting of funds to fighters according to need and size of family 22nd Rabīʿ II - 9th February
296	615	Ahmad Suleimān Reply to Letter 614, agreeing to payment according to merit 22nd Rabīʿ II - 9th February

Volume 4

Page	No.	Recipient – Subject matter – Dates
		1302 - 1885
297	616	Ahmad Suleimān Reply, emphasising accurate accounting of troops and payment Before 23rd Rabīʿ II - before 10th February
299	617	al-Tāhir al-Majdhūb Approval of wording of incantation, order to read Rātib and Qurʾān, how to become a companion 24th Rabīʿ II - 11th February
302	618	[From Ahmad Suleimān] Requests Mahdi's return to Omdurman from Karari, from where northern expedition departed 27th Rabīʿ II - 14th February
304	619	Ahmad Suleimān Reply to Letter 618, promising swift return, referring other issues to Khalīfa ʿAbdullāhi 27th Rabīʿ II - 14th February
305	620	[From Ahmad Suleimān] Recommends distributing slaves from Khartoum among army units 28th Rabīʿ II - 15th February
306	621	Khalīfa ʿAbdullāhi Agreement with suggestion on slaves [see Letter 620], orders distribution 28th Rabīʿ II - 15th February
307	622	Officers and troops of the English [Relief Expedition] Call for surrender, promise of pardon, otherwise death awaits 29th Rabīʿ II - 16th February

Volume 4

Page	No.	Recipient – Subject matter – Dates
		1302 – 1885
309	623	His beloved and intimate elite Condolences on the martyrdom of certain Anṣār 29th Rabīʿ II – 16th February
313	624	Ibrāhīm Hamdūk Scorn for recipient's not following the Mahdīa, urges rapid involvement Rabīʿ II – 19th Jan–16th Feb
314	625	Ahmad Suleimān Requests approval of payment to Ismāʿīl Daūd and his group from Beit al-Māl Rabīʿ II – 19th Jan–16th Feb
315	626	Ahmad Suleimān Agrees that total revenue of 30,000 riyals to be distributed among brigades of the three khulafāʾ Rabīʿ II – 19th Jan–16th Feb
317	627	Khalīfa ʿAbdullāhi and Khalīfa Sharīf Refuses request to make Muhammad Suleimān an amīr, saying he is too busy as a scribe Rabīʿ II – 19th Jan–16th Feb
318	628	Muhammad Ahmad Abū-Shūq Ahmad Suleimān to return escaped slave from Beit al-Māl Rabīʿ II – 19th Jan–16th Feb
319	629	Followers of Ahmad Abū-Shūq Orders change of name from Shūk ["thorns"] to Shūq ["longing"] on pain of 20 lashes Rabīʿ II – 19th Jan–16th Feb

Volume 4

Page	No.	Recipient – Subject matter - Dates
		1302 - 1885
320	630	[From Fadlallah Ahmad Idrīs] Appeal for help in reclaiming money and property from Beit al-Māl After 29th Rabīʿ II - after 16th February
322	631	Ahmad Suleimān Orders investigation into claim [see Letter 630] and pay the family a regular salary After 29th Rabīʿ II - after 16th February
323	632	ʿOsmān Digna Appointment of al-Hassan Ahmad al-Badawi Hāshi as amīr among the Beja 2nd Jumāda I - 18th February
324	633	[From Ahmad Suleimān] Informs that he is sending maid to the wife of Abū-al-Saʿūd on request 8th Jumāda I - 24th February
325	634	Ahmad Suleimān Reply to Letter 633, expressing satisfaction, calling for workers to repair shields and mint money 8th Jumāda I - 24th February
327	635	[From Ahmad Suleimān] Asks for ruling on donation of a daughter as a gift 9th Jumāda I - 25th February
328	636	Ahmad Suleimān Conveys complaints about favouritism towards Ashrāf, approves proposals on Khartoum housing 9th Jumāda I - 25th February

Volume 4

Page	No.	Recipient – Subject matter - Dates
		1302 - 1885
330	637	[From Aḥmad Suleimān] Query on appropriate allocations for the blind 9th Jumāda I - 25th February
332	638	Aḥmad Suleimān Reply to Letter 637, endorsing subsidies and advocating that the blind avoid begging 9th Jumāda I - 25th February
333	639	[From Muḥammad Bashīr, Yūsuf Suleimān, etc.] Complaint about greed of 24 blind people demanding excessive allocations 9th Jumāda I - 25th February
335	640	His beloved and intimate elite [i.e. the indigent blind people] States that the home provided for them is sufficient, discourages begging 9th Jumāda I - 25th February
336	641	[From Bābikr walad al-Raīs 'Omar] Complaint about seizure and looting of home in Khartoum, requests compensation 8th Jumāda I - 24th February
337	642	Aḥmad Suleimān Asks for investigation into substance of Letter 641 10th Jumāda I - 26th February
338	643	Bābikr walad al-Raīs 'Omar Reply to Letter 461, notifying recipient that investigation is underway 10th Jumāda I - 26th February

Volume 4

Page	No.	Recipient – Subject matter - Dates
		1302 - 1885
339	644	Khalīfa ʿAbdullāhi Delays caused by disobedience, calls for punishment of those who abuse women of Khartoum 10th Jumāda I - 26th February
342	645	Ahmad Muhammad al-Jārkūk, etc. Formal pardon, notification that his family is to be returned and given subsidies under Ismāʿīl Ahmad 11th Jumāda I - 27th February
345	646	Ahmad Suleimān Pardon of al-Jārkūk family, has asked to marry daughter of Abū-Bakr al-Jārkūk 11th Jumāda I - 27th February
346	647	Khalīfa ʿAbdullāhi Surviving members of al-Jārkūk family to be incoporated under Ismāʿīl ibn Ahmad Shadar al-Kheiri 11th Jumāda I - 27th February
347	648	ʿAbd-al-Rahmān al-Nujūmi and his brother Abū-Girja Refers to flight of British from Abū-Tulayh [Abu Klea], new force to relieve Sennār under Muhammad ʿAbd-al-Karīm 12th Jumāda I - 28th February
349	649	ʿAbd-al-Rahmān al-Nujūmi and his brother Abū-Girja Divert ammunition from ʿAli Saʿad Faraj to Muhammad al-Kheir to fight off British advance 12th Jumāda I - 28th February

Volume 4

Page	No.	Recipient – Subject matter - Dates
		1302 - 1885
351	650	All the beloved in the Faith, etc. Blesses appointment of Muhammad al-Tayyib al-Suleihābi as local amīr 12th Jumāda I - 28th February
352	651	Tribes of Rufā'a, Jaheina, etc. [on the Blue Nile] Scolding for inter-clan fighting, sends arbiter to rule on disputes After 12th Jumāda I - after 28th February
354	652	Muhammad Suleimān Join forces with Muhammad Khalīl and Muhammad 'Abd-al-Karīm of Sennār 15th Jumāda I - 3rd March
355	653	Hamid al-Nīl Hāmid Order to vacate home to make room for arsenal 17th Jumāda I - 5th March
356	654	His beloved muhājirūn [migrants] and Ansār Urges patience in times of difficulty, pardon for Muhammad Babikr whose daughter Mahdi married 19th Jumāda I - 7th March
358	655	Muhammad al-Kheir 'Abdallah Khojali Requests him to look after Nasīm ibn Adawi 20th Jumāda I - 8th March
359	656	Ansār heading towards Sennār Advice and instructions for contingent led by Muhammad 'Abd-al-Karīm 21st Jumāda I - 9th March

Volume 4

Page	No.	Recipient – Subject matter - Dates
		1302 - 1885
361	657	Muhammad Suleimān Adds footnote to letter prior to departure of Muhammad ʿAbd-al-Karīm and Ahmad al-Mukāshfi to Sennār 21st Jumāda I - 9th March
362	658	All the beloved and favoured khulafāʾ Approved distribution of loot by Ahmad al-Makāshi to followers prior to march on Sennār After 21st Jumāda I - after 9th March
364	659	His beloved Ansār Warning about money and fame as distractions from God's path, derides ʿulamāʾ 23rd Jumāda I - 11th March
370	660	[From Idrīs Muhammad Dawalīb and his brothers] Seeks permission to bring family from Jebel al-Harāza with laissez-passer for Hamdān Abū-ʿAnja After 28th Jumāda I - after 16th March
371	661	Idrīs Muhammad Dawalīb and his brothers Reply to Letter 660, approving request, asks for wife for Khalīfa Dirdīri, son of Muhammad Dawalīb 28th Jumāda I - 16th March
372	662	Hamdān Abū-ʿAnja Appointment as ʿāmil over Jebel Tagalia district, clarifies boundaries, urges consultations 29th Jumāda I - 17th March

Volume 4

Page	No.	Recipient – Subject matter - Dates
		1302 - 1885
376	663	Aḥmad Suleimān Reply, on bad financial situation, saying to ignore drought as only God provides Jumāda I - 17th Feb-18th March
378	664	Maḥmūd ʿIssa Zāʾid Sent Anṣār from Omdurman to fight Abyssinians, pledge to defeat Ṣāliḥ al-Takrūri 2nd Jumāda II - 20th March
380	665	Muḥammad Suleimān Approves content of Khalīfa ʿAbdullāhi's letter to Abū-Sinn clan, surrender to Muḥammad ʿOsmān Khālid 2nd Jumāda II - 20th March
381	666	[From Muḥammad Suleimān] Requests ruling on manumission of female slave 2nd Jumāda II - 20th March
382	667	Muḥammad Suleimān Reply to Letter 666, stating no change in status possible unless enslaved since Mahdīa began 2nd Jumāda II - 20th March
383	668	Commander of the Sennār expedition Criticism of attacks on local people, cites Abū-ʿAnja as role model After 2nd Jumāda II - after 20th March
385	669	Maḥmūd ʿAbd-al-Qādir Appointment of Hamdān Abū-ʿAnja as General Commander of Tagali, al-Dāyir and Gādir 5th Jumāda II - 23rd March

99

Volume 4

Page	No.	Recipient – Subject matter - Dates
		1302 - 1885
387	670	Hamdān Abū-'Anja Mahmūd 'Abd-al-Qādir instructed to assist, urges co-operation 5th Jumāda II - 23rd March
388	671	'Abd-al-Rahmān al-Nujūmi and Muhammad 'Osmān Abū-Girja Details of troop movements, Muhammad al-Kheir to collect zakāt and send regular supplies 5th Jumāda II - 23rd March
391	672	'Abd-al-Rahmān al-Nujūmi and Muhammad 'Osmān Abū-Girja Various instructions on Dongola campaign 5th Jumāda II - 23rd March
393	673	Muhammad al-Kheir 'Abdallah Khojali Order to assist Dongola expedition, defers advice on dealing with Aswan and southern Egypt 5th Jumāda II - 23rd March
395	674	'Ali Sa'ad Faraj Expedition to relieve Dongola, order to report to Omdurman with al-Nūr Angara 5th Jumāda II - 23rd March
397	675	Special officials and judges Confirms judicial ruling on land dispute 5th Jumāda II - 23rd March
398	676	Tāj al-Dīn, the sons of al-Mak 'Osmān, the sons of Yūsuf, etc. Order to follow local 'āmil Muhammad al-Mak Nāsir and besiege Sennār 6th Jumāda II - 24th March

Volume 4

Page	No.	Recipient – Subject matter - Dates
		1302 - 1885
401	677	al-Nūr Muhammad Angara Intention to liberate Dongola, instruction to return to Omdurman with all but Muhammad al-Badawi al-Siddīq 6th Jumāda II - 24th March
402	678	Muhammad al-Dawi al-Sādiq al-Kināni Order to accompany Shāmi Habāni on Dongola expedition 6th Jumāda II - 24th March
403	679	Mahmūd 'Abd-al-Qādir [in Kordofan] Refers to famine at Omdurman, orders handover of sorghum from Rahma Manūfal to Khalīfa 'Abdullāhi 6th Jumāda II - 24th March
406	680	Muhammad Khalīl Details of zakāt collection from various clans under al-Bashīr Taha 6th Jumāda II - 24th March
409	681	Mustafa 'Ali Hadal Order to settle disappointing dispute with 'Awad-al-Karīm al-Kāfūt 7th Jumāda II - 25th March
410	682	All his beloved Order to pay fares for river-crossings 8th Jumāda II - 26th March
412	683	[No recipient identified] Complaint of Ibrāhīm Adlan about demands made by brigade commanders 9th Jumāda II - 27th March

101

Volume 4

Page	No.	Recipient – Subject matter – Dates
		1302 – 1885
413	684	All followers and Ansār Organisation of rent from shops, mills, etc. for Beit al-Māl 9th Jumāda II – 27th March
414	685	Hamdān Abū-'Anja Pleasure at good conduct of troops, need judge's help in practising according to Mahdi's words 9th Jumāda II – 27th March
416	686	Ahmad Suleimān Offer of advice 9th Jumāda II – 27th March
417	687	[No recipient identified] Cites decree of Prophet that wealth of government and rich householders goes to Beit al-Māl After 9th Jumāda II – after 27th March
418	688	All his deputies Instructs officials to pass fair judgements, obeying orders of Khalīfa 'Abdullāhi and other leaders 10th Jumāda II – 28th March
422	689	All his companions and aides Lecture on concord within community, strict advice on Beit al-Māl property and how spent 14th Jumāda II – 1st April
424	690	Those leaving besieged Khartoum Loot from the city insufficient for Ansār needs, requiring extra from Berber 21st Jumāda II – 8th April

Volume 4

Page	No.	Recipient – Subject matter – Dates
		1302 – 1885
426	691	al-Majdhūb Hussein Appointment as ʿāmil over Dāgūri area on request of al-Nūr ibn al-Fuqara al-Jabarti 22nd Jumāda II – 9th April
427	692	Hamdān Abū-ʿAnja Informs of ʿAsākir Abū-Kalām's arrival, approves quarantining of smallpox victims 23rd Jumāda II – 10th April
430	693	Hamdān Abū-ʿAnja Reply, praising him for co-operation with Mahmūd ʿAbd-al-Qādir 24th Jumāda II – 11th April
432	694	Ahmad al-Nūr Fixes meeting with maternal uncle, ʿAli Saʿad, in charge of Metemma 29th Jumāda II – 16th April
433	695	ʿAli Bakhīt Chastises him for preventing Khalīfa ʿAbdullāhi taking sorghum from Kordofan 29th Jumāda II – 16th April
435	696	The people of Berber and Dongola Recycled material [using Letters 383 and 133], adding order to obey Muhammad al-Kheir 29th Jumāda II – 16th April
441	697	ʿAbd-al-Rahmān al-Nujūmi and Muhammad ʿOsmān Abū-Girja States that he has met requests for ammunition and expenses, wait for signal to travel 29th Jumāda II – 16th April

Volume 4

Page	No.	Recipient – Subject matter - Dates
		1302 - 1885
443	698	al-Hassan ʿOsmān and Mirghani Muhammad Sālih Join forces under Muhammad al-Kheir to attack Dongola, supplied with troops by al-Nujūmi 29th Jumāda II or 11th Rajab - 16th or 27th April
445	699	Muhammad al-Tayyib al-Basīr Could not send anything earlier owing to poverty of Beit al-Māl, now sending 150 riyals Jumāda II - 19th Mar-16th April
446	700	Khalīfa ʿAbdullāhi Order to ensure Abū-ʿAnja returns property to Manah clan After Jumāda II - after 17th April
448	701	al-Hassan Ahmad ʿOmar Baqādi Commiseration at loss of Amīna Ahmad ʿOmar Baqādi 3rd Rajab - 19th April
450	702	Muhammad al-Tayyib Qamr al-Dīn al-Majdhūb Grants permission to return home 4th Rajab - 20th April
452	703	Muhammad al-Kheir ʿAbdallah Khojali Appointment of Idrīs Suleimān as amīr of the al-Nafʿāb under his command 5th Rajab - 21st April
453	704	The Nafʿāb clan Appointment of Idrīs Suleimān as their amīr 5th Rajab - 21st April

Volume 4

Page	No.	Recipient – Subject matter - Dates
		1302 - 1885
454	705	Mahmūd 'Abd-al-Qādir Forwards presentation from Muhammad Ahmad Shaddād for consideration 5th Rajab - 21st April
455	706	Hamdān Abū-'Anja Reply, commenting on violent mutiny by al-Juma' clan 7th Rajab - 23rd April
458	707	Mustafa Yāwir Rebuke for supporting infidels and killing Muslims, pardon for surrender and repentance 7th Rajab - 23rd April
461	708	His Ansār and aides in Metemma Ban on molestation of woman whose husband is in Egypt, refers to earlier decree 10th Rajab - 26th April
462	709	All his beloved in God Declaration of pardon for daughter and family of al-Zubeir Rahma 10th Rajab - 26th April
463	710	Muhammad al-Kheir 'Abdallah Khojali New deployment of recipient to Dongola with reinforcements, al-Nujūmi stays at Metemma 11th Rajab - 27th April
465	711	al-Tāhir Tātāi and 'Abd-al-Qādir al-Tarīfi Approves force to Galābāt in consultation with Muhammad Arbāb 12th Rajab - 28th April

Volume 4

Page	No.	Recipient – Subject matter – Dates
		1302 - 1885
467	712	Muhammad Bābikr al-Suleihābi Appointment as successor to Muhammad al-Tayyib al-Suleihābi 12th Rajab - 28th April
469	713	'Abdallah Abū-Sinn and Tātāi wa al-Tarīfi Praise for information on Abyssinians, maintain siege of al-Jīra under Ahmad al-Buseiri 12th Rajab - 28th April
471	714	'Ali Munīr Refers dispute for adjudication with help of a judge 13th Rajab - 29th April
472	715	Sa'īd walad Bata and family Appointment as regional leader under brigade of Muhammad Abd-al-Karīm 14th Rajab - 30th April
473	716	al-'Ajab 'Ali Taha Abū-Jinn Annulment of marriage of a woman, order not to harrass her 19th Rajab - 5th May
474	717	[From al-Tayyib al-Banāni] Moroccan trader arrived at Berber, lost goods to looters, relative enslaved 5th Rajab - 21st April
476	718	Muhammad al-Kheir 'Abdallah Khojali Refers complaint [see Letter 717] and orders release of Moroccan's relative 20th Rajab - 6th May

Volume 4

Page	No.	Recipient – Subject matter – Dates
		1302 - 1885
477	719	[From Muḥammad al-Kheir ʿAbdallāh Khojali to Aḥmad Muḥammad ʿAbdallāh Khojali] Passes on order to free Moroccan's relative 18th Shaʿbān - 3rd June
478	720	Muḥammad ʿAbd-al-Karīm Orders inventory of sorghum stocks, more plentiful than in Omdurman 21st Rajab - 7th May
479	721	Aḥmad Suleimān Notification of pardon for Aḥmad Abū-al-Qāsim 22nd Rajab - 8th May
480	722	Muḥammad al-Kheir ʿAbdallāh Khojali Sending Aḥmad Hāshim and his son Muḥammad, as requested 22nd Rajab - 8th May
481	723	The people of Fez Introduction of Mahdīa, centrality of Qurʾān and Sunna, values of jihād, suggested local leader 22nd Rajab - 8th May
489	724	His beloved in God [in North-West Africa] General summons to people of the Maghreb, intention to conquer other countries 22nd Rajab - 8th May
496	725	ʿAbd-al-Raḥmān al-Nujūmi States that victims of smallpox epidemic are martyrs 23rd Rajab - 9th May

107

Volume 4

Page	No.	Recipient – Subject matter - Dates
		1302 - 1885
498	726	ʿAbd-al-Rahmān al-Nujūmi and Muhammad ʿOsmān Abū-Girja Condolences on death of Fadhalu Ahmad 24th Rajab - 10th May

Volume 5

Vol 5		272 letters (10th May - 22nd June 1885)
Page	No.	Recipient – Subject matter – Dates

1302 - 1885

Page	No.	
1	727	Muhammad al-Kheir 'Abdallah Khojali Debts owed by men on Dongola expedition cancelled, Hussein Khalīfa 'āmil of Egyptian districts 24th Rajab - 10th May
4	728	al-Hassan 'Osmān and Mīrghani Muhammad Suwār al-Dahab Pleased with prompt acceptance of Dongola mission and their approval of al-Nujūmi and Muhammad al-Kheir 24th Rajab - 10th May
6	729	The kin of Fadhalu Ahmad Condolences on death of Fadhalu Ahmad, Shāyib Ahmad appointed in his place 24th Rajab - 10th May
8	730	Muhammad al-Kheir 'Abdallah Khojali Reply, instructing dismissal of Ahmad Hamza, praise for Dongola preparations 24th Rajab - 10th May
10	731	Muhammad al-Kheir 'Abdallah Khojali Decision to drop one third of debt owed by people of Berber and Ja'aliyīn incurred buying slave women 25th Rajab - 11th May
12	732	Muhammad al-Ghāli 'Abd-al-Salām [in Fez] Nomination by followers as regional official for Fez, authority to receive allegiances to Mahdīa 25th Rajab - 11th May

Volume 5

Page	No.	Recipient – Subject matter - Dates
		1302 - 1885
15	733	Ibrāhīm al-Sanūsi al-Hassan, Muhammad ʿAbd-al-Salām, etc. Friendly reply, referring to appointment of Muhammad al-Ghāli as amīr of Marrakesh 25th Rajab - 11th May
17	734	Ahmad Suleimān Importance of correctly copying the Rātib 26th or 29th Rajab - 12th or 15th May
18	735	ʿAjiba bint Bāʾikr Authority to marry her daughter to whomever she pleases 27th Rajab - 13th May
19	736	Ahmad Suleimān Order to Beit al-Māl employee to return illegally seized ram 27th Rajab - 13th May
20	737	All his beloved Supporters of the Faith Refers to complaint by woman, orders relatives to stop harrassing her 27th Rajab - 13th May
21	738	Muhammad al-Kheir ʿAbdallah Khojali Request of Muhammad Ahmad Jalāl-al-Dīn al-Majdhūb to appoint brother as amīr, orders consultations 27th Rajab - 13th May
22	739	His beloved ones, agents and deputies Reqest for help by a woman, order that no-one may harrass her 27th Rajab - 13th May

110

Volume 5

Page	No.	Recipient – Subject matter - Dates
		1302 - 1885
23	740	al-Hassan ibn Muhammad ibn ʿAbd-al-Rahmān and [the people of] Fez Rehearsal of message to people of Morocco [see Letters 723 and 732], preparing for invasion of Egypt 28th Rajab - 14th May
26	741	Idrīs ʿAwād Order to divorce a woman recipient married despite her opposition Rajab - 17th April-16th May
27	742	Ahmad Abū-ʿAli Appointment in charge of al-ʿIlaiqāt under authority of Hussein Khalīfa 1st Shaʿbān - 17th May
29	743	Hamdān Abū-ʿAnja Compulsory purchase of grain from Jawāmʿa tribe for general distribution 2nd Shaʿbān - 18th May
33	744	Hawāzama tribe and clan of Nawāy Deifallah Order to repent after mutiny and disobedience, offering pardon for surrender After 2nd Shaʿbān - after 18th May
35	745	Mustafa ʿAli Hadal and ʿAwad al-Karīm Kāfūt Sent envoys to accept surrender of Kassala, requests lists of captured weapons 3rd Shaʿbān - 19th May

Volume 5

Page	No.	Recipient – Subject matter - Dates
		1302 - 1885
37	746	Ahmad 'Iffat [mudīr of Taka], Faraj Azāz, etc. Notice that envoy en route to accept their surrender, offers pardon and safe conduct 3rd Sha'bān - 19th May
40	747	al-Hassan Ibrāhīm Zahrā, etc. Appointment as envoys to accept surrender of Kassala, orders on collection of loot and weapons 3rd Sha'bān - 19th May
43	748	al-Hassan Ibrāhīm Zahrā, etc. Demobilisation of government troops native to Kassala 3rd Sha'bān - 19th May
44	749	al-Tāhir al-Tātāi and 'Abdallah al-Trīfi Orders co-operation with Beit al-Māl officer in collection of zakāt 3rd Sha'bān - 19th May
45	750	al-Hassan Ibrāhīm Zahrā, etc. Adds 'Abdallah Abū-Bakr al-Majdhūb to Kassala delegation as he knows region and language 3rd Sha'bān - 19th May
46	751	Muhammad al-Kheir 'Abdallah Khojali Approves request of Suleimān Garjāj and Sa'ad Sālim to join 'Ali Sa'ad 3rd Sha'bān - 19th May
47	752	Ahmad Suleimān Requests return of property of al-Musharraf Muhammad 3rd Sha'bān - 19th May

Volume 5

Page	No.	Recipient – Subject matter – Dates
		1302 - 1885
48	753	Muhammad Abū-Bakr Ja'far al-Mīrghani Reply, praising him for role at Kassala, details of surrender delegation 3rd Sha'bān - 19th May
49	754	al-'Awad, Chief Clerk at al-Taka State of Islam under "Turks", asks him to hand over Taka to delegation immediately 3rd Sha'bān - 19th May
51	755	'Abdallah Abū-Bakr al-Majdhūb Appointment as member of delegation to Kassala, 'Osmān Digna notified accordingly 3rd Sha'bān - 19th May
53	756	Mahmūd 'Abd-al-Qādir Ansār migrating to Omdurman without permission, now persuaded to return home 3rd Sha'bān - 19th May
55	757	'Osmān Digna Briefing on Kassala situation, delegation to consult with him 3rd Sha'bān - 19th May
58	758	[From al-Tayyib al-Banāni and Idrīs Abū-Ghālib] Heading to Morocco to spread the call, armed with Mahdi's proclamations, requests transport 4th Sha'bān - 20th May
60	759	Muhammad al-Kheir 'Abdallah Khojali Notification of al-Tayyib al-Banāni mission, orders to provide appropriate equipment 4th Sha'bān - 20th May

Volume 5

Page	No.	Recipient – Subject matter – Dates
		1302 – 1885
61	760	[From Muhammad al-Kheir to Ahmad Muhammad ʿAbdallah Khojali] Relays Mahdi's orders [see Letter 759] 18th Shaʿbān – 3rd June
62	761	al-Khawāja Georgios Salīb and Butrus Salīb [Egyptian Copts] Calls on them to convert to Islam like their brother, warning of intention to conquer Egypt 6th Shaʿbān – 22nd May
64	762	[No recipient identified] Reports revelations from holy man about fall of Sennār and march on Dongola After 7th Shaʿbān after 23rd May
66	763	Qāḍi al-Islam Ahmad ʿAli Forgiveness of unintentional actions, statement that handwriting has same value as official seal 8th Shaʿbān – 24th May
67	764	Muhammad ʿAbd-al-Karīm Request to look after relatives 10th Shaʿbān – 26th May
69	765	ʿOsmān Digna Variant of Letter 757, adding call to treat townspeople of Kassala gently, inventory loot and guns 10th Shaʿbān – 26th May
71	766	ʿAbd-al-Rahmān al-Qurāshi Intercedes on behalf of a woman who seeks forgiveness from recipient 10th Shaʿbān – 26th May

114

Volume 5

Page	No.	Recipient – Subject matter - Dates
		1302 - 1885
72	767	Mustafa ʿAli Hadal, etc. [Copy of Letter 745, with minor amendments] 10th Shaʿbān - 26th May
74	768	al-Hassan Ibrāhīm Zahrā, etc. [Copy of Letter 747] 10th Shaʿbān - 26th May
77	769	The people of Qeirā and Qomā Relates story of his Mahdism, appointment of Muhammad Jibrīl as local amīr 11th Shaʿbān - 27th May
80	770	al-Sayyid Muhammad ʿOsmān al-Mīrghani Chastises him for disregarding several letters, urges repentance and migration with Hussein Zahrā 11th Shaʿbān - 27th May
83	771	All his agents and Ansār Permission to salvage a sunken boat at Berber 11th Shaʿbān - 27th May
84	772	His beloved Muhammad ʿAbd-al-Qādir and his brother al-Hāj Sarfi Muhammad Reply, noting their status as hostages of British, comparing them to Christian captives who converted 11th Shaʿbān - 27th May
87	773	His beloved Muhammad ʿAbd-al-Qādir and his brother al-Hāj Sarfi Muhammad Rejects request that they be exchanged with European and Coptic prisoners 11th Shaʿbān - 27th May

Volume 5

Page	No.	Recipient – Subject matter - Dates
		1302 - 1885
90	774	Agent of Lord Wolseley and all his troops Call for surrender, comment that converted prisoners dearer to him than his own kinsmen in Dongola 11th Sha'bān - 27th May
92	775	All the tribes of the southern mountains Appointment of Muhammad Ahmad al-Suleihābi to replace Atta al-Manān al-Suleihābi 11th Sha'bān - 27th May
94	776	His beloved believers in God and his Book [at Marrakesh] Copy of Letter 42, adding family tree, al-Tayyib Ahmad to be local official [copies sent to West Africa] 11th Sha'bān - 27th May
98	777	Bashīr Mustafa Jibrān Reply, noting appointment over al-'Ashābāb, Hussein Khalīfa over the Abābda 12th Sha'bān - 28th May
100	778	al-Munshatih Karrār [Copy of Letter 777] 12th Sha'bān - 28th May
102	779	Hussein Khalīfa Appointment over the Abābda of Egypt, instructs him to head north 12th Sha'bān - 28th May
104	780	Hussein Khalīfa [Variant of Letter 779] 12th Sha'bān - 28th May

Volume 5

Page	No.	Recipient – Subject matter - Dates
		1302 - 1885
106	781	ʿAbd-al-Rahmān al-Nujūmi and those with him Appointment of Muhammad al-Kheir as leader of Dongola expedition 12th or 17th Shaʿbān - 28th May or 2nd June
108	782	al-Tayyib al-Manāni Appointment as agent in charge of Marrakesh under superior at Fez, gives text of bayʿa 13th Shaʿbān - 29th May
109	783	Muhammad al-Kheir ʿAbdallah Khojali Order to arrange travel of family to Omdurman at Beit al-Māl's expense 13th Shaʿbān - 29th May
110	784	ʿAbd-al-Rahmān al-Nujūmi Referral of complaint from a woman demanding justice 13th Shaʿbān - 29th May
111	785	All his beloved in God, agents, deputies and Ansār Pardons named women and forbids interfering with them 13th Shaʿbān - 29th May
112	786	[From al-Muddathir Ibrāhīm al-Hijjāz] Inquires about aspects of prayer and prostration 13th Shaʿbān - 29th May
113	787	al-Muddathir Ibrāhīm al-Hijjāz Reply to Letter 786, answering queries 15th Shaʿbān - 31st May

Volume 5

Page	No.	Recipient – Subject matter – Dates
		1302 - 1885
114	788	Muhammad ʿAbd-al-Karīm, his agent at Sennār Asks him to take care of al-Tayyib Suleihābi, calls for renewed focus on Sennār, sending ammunition 16th Shaʿbān - 1st June
117	789	Ansār heading to besiege Dongola Order to win over the people of Dongola and look after his relatives, descendants of al-Hāj Sharīf 14th or 17th Shaʿbān - 30th May or 2nd June
118	790	People of Jebel Najīli and Sodari Appointment of Hamdān ibn al-Mak Bashīr as local leader 17th Shaʿbān - 2nd June
121	791	People of Jebel Qabā and Kafāt Appointment of ʿAli Mustafa as local amīr under Muhammad Jibrīl, call for conversion 17th Shaʿbān - 2nd June
124	792	Muhammad al-Kheir ʿAbdallah Khojali Look after family of Jalāl al-Dīn, returning after seeking Mahdi's counsel 17th Shaʿbān - 2nd June
125	793	ʿAbd-al-Rahmān al-Nujūmi and [Muhammad ʿOsmān] Abū-Girja Reply, promising 50,000 riyals to ease difficulties of the mujāhidīn 17th Shaʿbān - 2nd June

Volume 5

Page	No.	Recipient – Subject matter – Dates
		1302 - 1885
127	794	Muhammad al-Kheir ʿAbdallah Khojali Hussein Khalīfa in charge of Abābda in Egypt, Abābda in Sudan under Berber authorities 18th Shaʿbān - 3rd June
129	795	Muhammad al-Kheir ʿAbdallah Khojali Confirmation of superiority of Ahmad Muhammad al-Kheir over ʿAbd-al-Rahmān Ziyād 18th Shaʿbān - 3rd June
130	796	Muhammad al-Kheir ʿAbdallah Khojali Reply, answering question on zakāt, notice of support to be expected from al-Nujūmi 18th Shaʿbān - 3rd June
133	797	Muhammad al-Kheir ʿAbdallah Khojali Refers to letter to Nujūmi urging move on Dongola without worrying about preparation or equipment 18th Shaʿbān - 3rd June
136	798	Hassan Abi-Sīdein Appointment with Bashīr Mustafa Jibrān as officials over al-ʿAshābāb under Hussein Khalīfa 18th Shaʿbān - 3rd June
137	799	Ahmad Muhammad al-Kheir Reply, noting news and referring to correspondence with Nujūmi and Muhammad al-Kheir 18th Shaʿbān - 3rd June

Volume 5

Page	No.	Recipient – Subject matter - Dates
		1302 - 1885
138	800	Muhammad ʿOsmān Abū-Girja and agent of ʿAli Saʿad Instructs both to remain in Metemma when army leaves for Dongola 18th Shaʿbān - 3rd June
140	801	Ansār beseiging Sennār Call to tighten siege until town falls, under leadership of ʿAbd-al-Karīm 18th Shaʿbān - 3rd June
143	802	Muhammad ʿOsmān Muhammad Farah States location and status of Bilāl Ramadān, asks him to return what was taken 18th Shaʿbān - 3rd June
145	803	Agents accompanying al-Nujūmi en route to Metemma Reiterates that the Khalīfa Sharīfs brigades are under Nujūmi's overall command 18th or 19th Shaʿbān - 3rd or 4th June
147	804	Abd-al-Halīm Musāʿid [Copy of Letter 803] 18th Shaʿbān - 3rd June
148	805	Ansār of al-Karrār's brigades Briefing on Dongola expedition, calling for rapid mobilisation 19th Shaʿbān - 4th June
154	806	al-Majdhūb Abū-Bakr Yūsuf Orders to accommodate ʿAbdullāhi al-Tayyib al-Majdhūb and followers, describes correct bayʿa 19th Shaʿbān - 4th June

Volume 5

Page	No.	Recipient – Subject matter - Dates
		1302 - 1885
155	807	Muhammad ʿOsmān Khālid Refers to interception of ten letters from Muhammad ʿOsmān al-Mirghani 22nd Shaʿbān - 7th June
157	808	Hamdān Abū-ʿAnja Reply, approving suggestions, urges motivation of local population to good deeds 22nd Shaʿbān - 7th June
160	809	All the Ansār and the beloved Ruling that river ports belong to Beit al-Māl, revenue to go to the army 22nd Shaʿbān - 7th June
163	810	ʿAwad al-Karīm Fadlallah Kāfūt Reply, confirming options: serve under [Mustafa] Hadal, under ʿOsmān Digna or come to Omdurman 22nd Shaʿbān - 7th June
165	811	Khalīfa Muhammad Sharīf Complaints from people of Bāra that order [at al- ʿObeid] to return loot not obeyed 22nd Shaʿbān - 7th June
167	812	His cousin, the deputy Muhammad Order to return illegally seized slaves 22nd Shaʿbān - 7th June
168	813	Hamdān Abū-ʿAnja Those holding Abū-Rūhein [double-barelled rifles] permitted to keep them, with some exceptions 22nd Shaʿbān - 7th June

Volume 5

Page	No.	Recipient – Subject matter – Dates
		1302 - 1885
169	814	The people of Khandaq Reply, accepting apology for following Mustafa Yāwir, accepting loyalty 22nd Shaʻbān - 7th June
171	815	All the Haderdawa, Halanqa, Beni Amir, Jaʻaliyīn, etc. Reply, refusing request to leave ʻOsmān Digna and follow al-Hassan Hāshi 22nd Shaʻbān - 7th June
173	816	Nuwāi Seifallah Reply, accepting repentance, orders support for Hamdān Abū-ʻAnja 22nd Shaʻbān - 7th June
174	817	Mahmūd ʻAbd-al-Qādir Refers complaint by a woman 22nd Shaʻbān - 7th June
175	818	[From Ahmad Suleimān] Obeying order to focus on Dongola force, specifics of funding to different brigades 23rd Shaʻbān - 8th June
177	819	Ahmad Suleimān Reply to Letter 818, congratulating him on his efforts 23rd Shaʻbān - 8th June
178	820	ʻOsmān Digna Instruction to hand on gifts to Beit al-Māl 23rd Shaʻbān - 8th June

Volume 5

Page	No.	Recipient – Subject matter – Dates
		1302 – 1885
179	821	All his agents and Anṣār Order not to harrass Muhammad ibn Amir, who has been given land and property 22nd Shaʿbān – 7th June
180	822	[From Ahmad Suleimān] Visited Ismāʿīl Daūd [relative of Mahdi's wife] and found him on death-bed, requests visit by Mahdi Before 24th Shaʿbān – before 9th June
181	823	Ahmad Suleimān Reply to Letter 822, ruling out visit to Khartoum, too busy visiting smallpox victims in Omdurman Before 24th Shaʿbān – before 9th June
182	824	[From Ahmad Suleimān] Death of Ismāʿīl Daūd, requests visit by Mahdi for funeral prayers Before 24th Shaʿbān – before 9th June
183	825	Ahmad Suleimān Reply to Letter 824, again refusing on grounds of illness, orders body to be brought over by boat Before 24th Shaʿbān – before 9th June
184	826	Ahmad Suleimān Orders Ismāʿīl Daūd's salary to go to his son Hamad al-Nīl Before 24th Shaʿbān – before 9th June
185	827	[From Ahmad Suleimān] Notifies of death of al-ʿUbeid Muhammad Saʿīd Before 24th Shaʿbān – before 9th June

Volume 5

Page	No.	Recipient – Subject matter – Dates
		1302 – 1885
186	828	Ahmad Suleimān Reply to Letter 827, with condolences Before 24th Sha'bān – before 9th June
187	829	People of al-Jībrīa Appointment of Rahma Muhammad Sa'īd in place of his brother al-'Ubeid Muhammad Sa'īd 24th Sha'bān – 9th June
188	830	Ahmad 'Abdallah Muhammad Nūr Garāfi Appointment as local amīr, orders him to catch up with al-Nujūmi heading for Dongola 24th Sha'bān – 9th June
189	831	Rahma Muhammad Sa'īd Appointment as agent over al-Jībrīa [see Letter 829] 24th Sha'bān – 9th June
190	832	Muhammad 'Osmān Khālid Orders those responsible for clash with Muhammad 'Abd-al-Karīm's faction to be sent to him 24th Sha'bān – 9th June
192	833	Muhammad 'Abd-al-Karīm Refers to letter from Muhammad 'Osmān Khālid over clash over zakāt, summons perpetrators 24th Sha'bān – 9th June
193	834	[From Muhammad Sāleh Sāti 'Ali] Describes a dream and requests interpretation 25th Sha'bān – 10th June

Volume 5

Page	No.	Recipient – Subject matter - Dates
		1302 - 1885
194	835	Muhammad Sāleh Sāti 'Ali Reply to Letter 834, saying disease and swelling in dream is proof of recipient's moral hypocrisy 25th Sha'bān - 10th June
196	836	Ahmad Suleimān Follow-up on instructions that port assets revert to Beit al-Māl [see Letter 809] 25th Sha'bān - 10th June
197	837	[From Muhammad 'Osmān 'Abdallah] Asks about retrospective collection of zakāt in Rufa'a region 26th or 28th Sha'bān - 11th or 13th June
199	838	Muhammad 'Osmān 'Abdallah Laws of Mahdīa and therefore zakāt collection back-dated to date of victory over Hicks [4 November 1883] 26th or 28th Sha'bān - 11th or 13th June
200	839	Muhammad Sāleh Sāti 'Ali Refers to withdrawal of "Turks" from Dongola, Muhammad al-Kheir ordered to return 26th Sha'bān - 11th June
202	840	al-Hussein Ibrāhīm Zahrā Pardon for 'Abd-al-Mājid Hamad 26th Sha'bān - 11th June
203	841	His representative at Sennār, Muhammad 'Abd-al-Karīm Try to evacuate relatives of 'Abd-al-Mājid Hamad Muhammad Khojali from Sennār 26th Sha'bān - 11th June

Volume 5

Page	No.	Recipient – Subject matter – Dates
		1302 - 1885
205	842	Dāwūd Muhammad Licence to be an imām as requested by ʿAbdallah ʿAwad-al-Karīm Abū-Sinn 26th Shaʿbān - 11th June
207	843	All the Ansār Order not to be disturbed during Ramadan, all questions to be referred to subordinates 29th Shaʿbān - 14th June
209	844	ʿOsmān Digna Permission for Muhammad ibn Mahmūd to visit father in the east, free of pursuit for debts 29th Shaʿbān - 14th June
210	845	His beloved [probably Muhammad Ahmad al-Badawi] Declaration that Mahdi's fifth of loot has been given away, values of poverty and humility Shaʿbān - 17th May-14th June
212	846	Muhammad Ahmad al-Badawi Warning against half-heartedness and weakness Shaʿbān - 17th May-14th June
213	847	Ahmad Suleimān Priority given to Dongola expedition, Mahdi suffering from kūfār [headache and dizziness] Shaʿbān - 17th May-14th June
214	848	The khulafāʾ Priority given to Dongola expedition, complaint of illness, Khalīfa ʿAbdullāhi his trusted deputy Shaʿbān - 17th May-14th June

Volume 5

Page	No.	Recipient – Subject matter – Dates
		1302 - 1885
215	849	Khalīfa ʿAbdullāhi Charges him as representative at Beit al-Māl meeting to discuss funding priorities Shaʿbān - 17th May-14th June
217	850	Khalīfa ʿAbdullāhi Importance of speeding up conquest of Sennār, supplies to be sent Shaʿbān - 17th May-14th June
218	851	Khalīfa ʿAbdullāhi Reply, rejecting proposal to investigate Ahmad Suleimān's conduct as head of Beit al-Māl Shaʿbān - 17th May-14th June
220	852	Muhammad al-Amīn Ahmad Appointment as agent in charge of western territories [Mali], under authority of Hayāt ibn Saʿīd Shaʿbān - 17th May-14th June
222	853	The people of Shinqīt [Mauretania] Basic introduction to Mahdīa, Muhammad Taqi al-Dīn to be local amīr [similar to Letter 723] Shaʿbān - 17th May-14th June
229	854	All the Ansār of the Faith Pardons Muhammad ʿAli al-Toam for carrying Gordon's letters to the English 1st Ramadan - 15th June

Volume 5

Page	No.	Recipient – Subject matter – Dates
		1302 - 1885
230	855	ʿAbd-al-Rahmān al-Nujūmi Refers to pardon of family of al-Zubeir Rahma [Letter 709], orders obedience and end to harrassment 1st Ramadan - 15th June
231	856	Mahmūd ʿAbd-al-Qādir Orders better consultation with his followers 1st Ramadan - 15th June
233	857	Ansār in Mahmūd ʿAbd-al-Qādir's brigade Call for obedience to their amīr Mahmūd ʿAbd-al-Qādir [see Letter 856] 1st Ramadan - 15th June
234	858	Johannes, Emperor of al-Habsha [Abyssinia] Explains Mahdīa as salvation of Islam, takeover of Sudan complete, calls for conversion 2nd Ramadan - 16th June
237	859	Muhammad Arbāb Reply, referring to earlier correspondence [Letter 711], urging cordiality and co-operation 2nd Ramadan - 16th June
239	860	Muhammad al-Malik Hamid, etc. Notes surrender of recipients as reported by Ibrāhīm al-Kāshif and Muhammad Sālih Sāti 2nd Ramadan - 16th June
241	861	The wāli [Governor] of Egypt Explanation of Mahdīa and recent events, rebuke for befriending infidels and heeding evil ʿulamāʾ 3rd Ramadan - 17th June

Volume 5

Page	No.	Recipient – Subject matter – Dates
		1302 - 1885
246	862	The 'ulamā' of Egypt Deterioration of Islamic world, hegemony of infidels, role of 'ulamā' in harming Sharī'a 3rd Ramadan - 17th June
251	863	The population of Egypt Details of conflict with "Turks" thus far, criticism for lack of support, intention to conquer Egypt 3rd Ramadan - 17th June
254	864	His deputies on earth Approves request to appoint Ahmad al-Rayah Dashīn as overseer of Wad Medani 5th Ramadan - 19th June
255	865	al-Hassan Ahmad al-Badawi Hāshi Concern over disagreements with 'Osmān Digna, orders settlement of dispute and obedience 6th Ramadan - 20th June
257	866	'Osmān Digna Request to take care of al-Hassan Ahmad al-Badawi [see Letter 865] 6th Ramadan - 20th June
259	867	Hayāt ibn Sa'īd Appointment as 'āmil over Sokoto, updates on appointment of Muhammad al-Amīn Ahmad in Mali 7th Ramadan - 21st June

Volume 5

Page	No.	Recipient – Subject matter - Dates
		1302 - 1885
262	868	Muhammad al-Tayyib al-Basīr, Muhammad Imām and brothers Refusal to permit followers to abandon jihād and return to their farms 7th Ramadan - 21st June
264	869	The director of the Beit al-Māl [Ahmad Suleimān] Order to return a maid of Nūr al-Jalīl's wife [postscript in different hand notes handover took place] [During 1302] - 22nd Oct 1884-22nd June 1885
265	870	Muhammad Nabawi Praise and instruction to be pious and detached from worldly affairs [During 1302] - 22nd Oct 1884-22nd June 1885
266	871	Khalīfa 'Abdullāhi Repentance of Sālih al-Makk, instruction that he be released [During 1302] - 22nd Oct 1884-22nd June 1885
267	872	al-Hassan Sa'ad al-'Abādi Order to go to Berber and join Muhammad al-Kheir [During 1302] - 22nd Oct 1884-22nd June 1885
269	873	al-Hāj 'Ali Muhammad Sālim Reply to request for money, agreeing but warning of worldy evils [During 1302] - 22nd Oct 1884-22nd June 1885

130

Volume 5

Page	No.	Recipient – Subject matter – Dates
		1302 – 1884-5
270	874	Ahmad Suleimān Praises some of his measures [During 1302] - 22nd Oct 1884-22nd June 1885
271	875	Ahmad Suleimān Commandeering of mules to pull artillery, camels to be offered as replacements [During 1302] - 22nd Oct 1884-22nd June 1885
272	876	Ahmad Suleimān Order to send slaves and money to al-Sayyid ʿAbd-al-Rāziq to build a house [During 1302] - 22nd Oct 1884-22nd June 1885
273	877	Ahmad Suleimān Slave and his daughter to be removed from an inheritance and handed over to a widow [During 1302] - 22nd Oct 1884-22nd June 1885
274	878	Taha Muhammad Boat to be returned to its owner, Ahmad Suleimān's orders to be obeyed [During 1302] - 22nd Oct 1884-22nd June 1885
275	879	The amnāʾ Orders return of loot taken from farm belonging to mother of a martyr [During 1302] - 22nd Oct 1884-22nd June 1885
276	880	The amnāʾ Requests consideration of an application [During 1302] - 22nd Oct 1884-22nd June 1885

Volume 5

Page	No.	Recipient – Subject matter – Dates
		1302 – 1884-5
277	881	al-Qurāshi ibn al-Sheikh al-Tayyib Approves his marriage and sends money [During 1302] - 22nd Oct 1884-22nd June 1885
278	882	The amnā' Requests that applicant be permitted to head south [During 1302] - 22nd Oct 1884-22nd June 1885
279	883	The amnā' Honour due to individual who fled the infidel and joined Mahdīa [During 1302] - 22nd Oct 1884-22nd June 1885
280	884	All companions and his beloved States that al-Nūr Ibrāhīm has settled his debt to the Christian [During 1302] - 22nd Oct 1884-22nd June 1885
281	885	[From Ismā'īl Ahmad] Asks for relatives to be listed among the elderly due Beit al-Māl pension [During 1302] - 22nd Oct 1884-22nd June 1885
282	886	Ahmad Suleimān Instructs that regular pensions be paid to Ismā'īl Ahmad [see Letter 885] [During 1302] - 22nd Oct 1884-22nd June 1885
283	887	[From Ahmad Muhammad Sharfi] Informs about death of Batūl bint al-Muqaddam, asks for advice on funeral [During 1302] - 22nd Oct 1884-22nd June 1885

Volume 5

Page	No.	Recipient – Subject matter – Dates
		1302 – 1884-5
284	888	Ahmad Suleimān Asks for body to be brought [see Letter 887] for funeral prayers, unless unable to cross to Omdurman [During 1302] - 22nd Oct 1884-22nd June 1885
285	889	Muhammad Sharīf Nūr al-Dā'im and sister Welcome, instruction not to rely on kinship and family connections [During 1302] - 22nd Oct 1884-22nd June 1885
287	890	Ahmad Suleimān Summons to meeting, refers to bliss experienced by martyrs [During 1302] - 22nd Oct 1884-22nd June 1885
288	891	[From al-Muddathir Ibrāhīm al-Hijjāz] Asks advice about marriage of a companion [During 1302] - 22nd Oct 1884-22nd June 1885
289	892	al-Muddathir Ibrāhīm al-Hijjāz Reply to Letter 891, approving marriage, outlining characteristics of a good wife [During 1302] - 22nd Oct 1884-22nd June 1885
290	893	His beloved Advice to maintain distance from this worthless world [During 1302] - 22nd Oct 1884-22nd June 1885
292	894	Khalīfa 'Abdullāhi Urges rebuilding of relationship with repentant Muhammad al-Tayyib al-Basīr [During 1302] - 22nd Oct 1884-22nd June 1885

Volume 5

Page	No.	Recipient – Subject matter - Dates
		1302 – 1884-5
293	895	Muhammad Fawzi Mahmūd Requests accommodation for certain Ashrāf [During 1302] - 22nd Oct 1884-22nd June 1885
294	896	ʿAli Saʿad [in charge at Metemma] Congratulations on marriage, noting that wives of Ansār who share hardships share status and merit [During 1302] - 22nd Oct 1884-22nd June 1885
295	897	al-Sheikh Tāha Bashīr Denies giving authority to re-marriage of divorced man, orders the man who lied to come to him [During 1302] - 22nd Oct 1884-22nd June 1885
296	898	Muhammad Suleimān Reply, to representation about a farm belonging to debtor [During 1302] - 22nd Oct 1884-22nd June 1885
297	899	[From ʿAbd-al-Qādir [Rudolf Slatin]] Complaint that no money received since arriving at Shāt, paying for own camels [During 1302] - 22nd Oct 1884-22nd June 1885
298	900	Ahmad Suleimān Refers Slatin's complains [see Letter 899], orders Beit al-Māl to make allowances [During 1302] - 22nd Oct 1884-22nd June 1885
299	901	Idrīs al-Sāyir [the jailer] Urges kindness to prisoners, worship should be more important than penal labour [During 1302] - 22nd Oct 1884-22nd June 1885

Volume 5

Page	No.	Recipient – Subject matter - Dates
		1302 – 1884-5
300	902	His beloved Ansār Commentary on Hadīth that Paradise surrounded by loathsome things [During 1302] - 22nd Oct 1884-22nd June 1885
303	903	The al-Basīr family Approves marriage of Ahmad al-Aghbash [During 1302] - 22nd Oct 1884-22nd June 1885
304	904	The al-Basīr family [Copy of Letter 903 with small variation] [During 1302] - 22nd Oct 1884-22nd June 1885
305	905	The beloved ones States that Mahdīa is not about titled rulers and hierarchy, Ansār to abandon personal ambition [During 1302] - 22nd Oct 1884-22nd June 1885
308	906	The beloved ones Poor and weak were the Prophet's best followers, urges Ansār to rise above gossip and bear abuse [During 1302] - 22nd Oct 1884-22nd June 1885
314	907	Ahmad Muhammad al-Fādni Praise for refusal to be appointed amīr, urging worship and piety [During 1302] - 22nd Oct 1884-22nd June 1885
315	908	al-Hāj 'Abdallah Refers to letter pledging sincere devotion, urges immediate migration [During 1302] - 22nd Oct 1884-22nd June 1885

Volume 5

Page	No.	Recipient – Subject matter – Dates
		1302 – 1884-5
316	909	The 'ulamā' of Rufā'a Refers to apostasy and repentance, call to avoid arrogance on basis of knowledge [During 1302] - 22nd Oct 1884-22nd June 1885
318	910	Muhammad Ṣālih Suwār al-Dahab and his brothers Appoints son to head local group, to be incorporated into brigade [During 1302] - 22nd Oct 1884-22nd June 1885
319	911	al-Khalīfa al-Sheikh Muhammad [Copy of Letter 910] [During 1302] - 22nd Oct 1884-22nd June 1885
320	912	[No recipient identified] Commentary on Hadīth praising the poor; their status in the after-life [During 1302] - 22nd Oct 1884-22nd June 1885
322	913	[No recipient identified] Commentary on Hadīth stressing reliance on God [During 1302] - 22nd Oct 1884-22nd June 1885
324	914	Taha 'Abd-al-Bāqi Emphasises importance of co-operation with each man's amīr [During 1302] - 22nd Oct 1884-22nd June 1885
325	915	Ahmad Suleimān Names a new-born baby: 'Abdallah al-Mubārak [During 1302] - 22nd Oct 1884-22nd June 1885

Volume 5

Page	No.	Recipient – Subject matter – Dates
		1302 – 1884-5
326	916	Ahmad Suleimān Praise for caring for Muhammad Saʿīd, order that he is to be given slaves [During 1302] – 22nd Oct 1884-22nd June 1885
327	917	Ahmad Suleimān Urges him to endure gossip and calumny [During 1302] – 22nd Oct 1884-22nd June 1885
329	918	Ahmad Suleimān Request to settle applicant's debt and pay him a salary [During 1302] – 22nd Oct 1884-22nd June 1885
330	919	Ahmad Suleimān Orders salaries to be paid to the families of Taha and his brother [During 1302] – 22nd Oct 1884-22nd June 1885
331	920	Khalīfa ʿAbdullāhi Approves request of Samīm tribe for help [During 1302] – 22nd Oct 1884-22nd June 1885
332	921	Khalīfa ʿAbdullāhi Refers representation from agents for his consideration [During 1302] – 22nd Oct 1884-22nd June 1885
333	922	Khalīfa ʿAbdullāhi Refers complaint [During 1302] – 22nd Oct 1884-22nd June 1885

Volume 5

Page	No.	Recipient – Subject matter - Dates
		1302 – 1884-5
334	923	Khalīfa 'Abdullāhi Requests return of property belonging to the late walad al-Karīf to a female applicant [During 1302] - 22nd Oct 1884-22nd June 1885
335	924	Muhammad Umm Baddah, etc. Criticism for fornication and dancing at expense of prayers and rituals, threatens punishment [During 1302] - 22nd Oct 1884-22nd June 1885
338	925	People of Jebel al-Kanak Criticism for dancing, drinking, taking snuff and eating pork, orders better religious observation [During 1302] - 22nd Oct 1884-22nd June 1885
340	926	'Abd-al-Bāqi Habīballah Punishment ordered (in consultation with Abū-Girja) for al-Wāliya tribespeople refusing to join his brigade [During 1302] - 22nd Oct 1884-22nd June 1885
342	927	The Wāliya tribe 'Abd-al-Bāqi Habīballah appointed to replace Sheikh al-Nayal, order to join his brigade [During 1302] - 22nd Oct 1884-22nd June 1885
344	928	Muhammad Nūr ibn Hasana and Hāshim ibn al-Zubeir Instruction to observe piety, proriety, patience and prayer [During 1302] - 22nd Oct 1884-22nd June 1885

Volume 5

Page	No.	Recipient – Subject matter – Dates
		1302 – 1884-5
345	929	Umarā', deputies, Ansār and village chiefs Permission granted to Jaāfra tribe to migrate en masse, prohibits harrassment [During 1302] - 22nd Oct 1884-22nd June 1885
346	930	Collectors of zakāt and loot Increasing number of complaints, orders them not to be violent or spy on people [During 1302] - 22nd Oct 1884-22nd June 1885
349	931	His beloved brothers, the umarā' Instruction to observe salāt al-jamā'a [communal prayers] [During 1302] - 22nd Oct 1884-22nd June 1885
351	932	Ansār of the Faith 'Abdullāhi al-Muslimāni to be sent to Egyptian territories with letter urging joining Mahdīa [During 1302] - 22nd Oct 1884-22nd June 1885
352	933	[No recipient identified] Asks that Khalīfa 'Abdullāhi be kept informed of subject under discussion [During 1302] - 22nd Oct 1884-22nd June 1885
353	934	His beloved and chosen ones Ordeals and tests are a blessing to purify the soul [During 1302] - 22nd Oct 1884-22nd June 1885
355	935	Muhammad al-Tayyib al-Basīr Order to report within the hour [During 1302] - 22nd Oct 1884-22nd June 1885

Volume 5

Page	No.	Recipient – Subject matter - Dates
		1302 – 1884-5
356	936	Muhammad al-Tayyib al-Basīr Reminder of the baseness of life [During 1302] - 22nd Oct 1884-22nd June 1885
357	937	Muhammad al-Mustafa ibn al-Imām States that there is no fault in making the hijra with women, a donkey and a servant [During 1302] - 22nd Oct 1884-22nd June 1885
358	938	[No recipient identified] Empty nature of present life in comparison with the after-life [During 1302] - 22nd Oct 1884-22nd June 1885
359	939	Muhammad al-Kheir 'Abdallah Khojali Request to obey the wishes of the converts as per earlier request [During 1302] - 22nd Oct 1884-22nd June 1885
360	940	Ahmad Hamdān al-'Araki Instruction to abandon named books and rely on the Qur'ān, the Hadīth and biographies of the Prophet [During 1302] - 22nd Oct 1884-22nd June 1885
361	941	Beloved ones Order to be purified by returning loot [During 1302] - 22nd Oct 1884-22nd June 1885
362	942	Muhammad ibn Rahmatallah Order to report for education, illness is usual for the chosen ones [During 1302] - 22nd Oct 1884-22nd June 1885

Volume 5

Page	No.	Recipient – Subject matter - Dates
		1302 – 1884-5
363	943	His beloved ones Urges them not to seek prestige or high office [During 1302] - 22nd Oct 1884-22nd June 1885
366	944	His beloved ones Call to follow new adherent Sabūn, abrogation of all religious books except the Qurʿān and Hadīth [During 1302] - 22nd Oct 1884-22nd June 1885
369	945	His companions and beloved ones Moral pep-talk about sowing seeds of fruit in the after-life, abandoning money and luxuries [During 1302] - 22nd Oct 1884-22nd June 1885
373	946	His companions and beloved ones Tests and ordeals are from God, call to endure malicious gossip [During 1302] - 22nd Oct 1884-22nd June 1885
375	947	ʿAli Muhammad al-Amīn al-Hindi, Hamad al-Nīl and Suleimān al-ʿUbeid Call for consensus and mutual affection among the people [During 1302] - 22nd Oct 1884-22nd June 1885
376	948	Amīna Muhammad Suleimān Instruction that the children and property of a certain woman should be cared for [During 1302] - 22nd Oct 1884-22nd June 1885
377	949	Muhammad al-Mādih the Praise-Singer Elevation to status of the Prophet's own poet, Hassān, also a member of the Mahdi's own household [During 1302] - 22nd Oct 1884-22nd June 1885

Volume 5

Page	No.	Recipient – Subject matter – Dates
		1302 – 1884-5
378	950	al-Aghbash ibn al-Basīr Presents horse as gift in commiseration for difficulties of making hijra [During 1302] - 22nd Oct 1884-22nd June 1885
379	951	Amir ibn al-Sheikh 'Omar al-Makāshfi Asks to consider claim by Ahmad 'Abdallah and family of Muhammad Ismā'īl [During 1302] - 22nd Oct 1884-22nd June 1885
380	952	Every companion and beloved one Interprets sūra of Qur'ān abour promise to the faithful, takes to mean his companions [During 1302] - 22nd Oct 1884-22nd June 1885
382	953	Ahmad Suleimān Reply, approving request of payment of slave maidens and gold to Beit al-Māl to settle debts [During 1302] - 22nd Oct 1884-22nd June 1885
383	954	Believers in Allah and in the Day of Judgement Absolute power of God, ordeals to be faced patiently, trust in God not sheikhs or the rich [During 1302] - 22nd Oct 1884-22nd June 1885
386	955	Khalīfa 'Abdullāhi Approval of proposal that al-Makāshfi's clan join the banner of Khalīfa Sharīf [During 1302] - 22nd Oct 1884-22nd June 1885
387	956	The beloved Urges pure belief in God, not to fear the enemy or its guns and bullets [During 1302] - 22nd Oct 1884-22nd June 1885

142

Volume 5

Page	No.	Recipient – Subject matter – Dates
		1302 – 1884-5
389	957	All brothers and companions Refers to previous warnings against worldliness, especially in connection with women [During 1302] - 22nd Oct 1884-22nd June 1885
391	958	My beloved Warning against jinx of high office for ambitious men, call to observe etiquette of entering a house [During 1302] - 22nd Oct 1884-22nd June 1885
393	959	Khalīfa ʿAbdullāhi Orders slave to be given to ʿIssa Bedran, a relative by marriage and veteran of Khartoum siege [During 1302] - 22nd Oct 1884-22nd June 1885
394	960	Khalīfa ʿAbdullāhi Orders release of ibn ʿArīf Sālih on representation of Muhammad Suleimān, orders arbitration into rivalry [During 1302] - 22nd Oct 1884-22nd June 1885
395	961	Khalīfa ʿAbdullāhi Release of applicant from prison, to be awarded remaining property free from harrassment [During 1302] - 22nd Oct 1884-22nd June 1885
396	962	Khalīfa ʿAbdullāhi Approves application to join al-Nujūmi's brigade, orders immediate implementation [During 1302] - 22nd Oct 1884-22nd June 1885
428	975	[No recipient identified] List of 105 members of al-Sharīf Hamad al-Nīl's clan [During 1302] - 22nd Oct 1884-22nd June 1885

Volume 5

Page	No.	Recipient – Subject matter – Dates
		1302 – 1884-5

429   976   Ahmad Suleimān
Orders salary to be paid to al-Nīl clan [see Letter 975], even if at expense of Mahdi's own family
[During 1302] - 22nd Oct 1884-22nd June 1885

430   977   Ahmad Suleimān
al-Muslimānīa [converts] to be given salaries and encouraged to attend majālis [meetings], notes on marriage to nuns
[During 1302] - 22nd Oct 1884-22nd June 1885

431   978   All companions
Permission for umarā' to pray separately with followers
[During 1302] - 22nd Oct 1884-22nd June 1885

432   979   Ibrāhīm Muhammad al-Dalīl
Correction of Rātib text, with additions
[During 1302] - 22nd Oct 1884-22nd June 1885

433   980   Ibrāhīm Muhammad al-Dalīl
Reply, agreeing to have copies made of the Rātib
[During 1302] - 22nd Oct 1884-22nd June 1885

434   981   Ibrāhīm Muhammad al-Dalīl
Clarifying number of repetitions (7 or 70) in corrected copy [see Letter 979]
[During 1302] - 22nd Oct 1884-22nd June 1885

435   982   [No recipient identified]
Muhammad Sharīf 'Abd-al-Hai to be amīr over Abū-Rakham village, under 'Abdullāhi Abū-Sinn
[During 1302] - 22nd Oct 1884-22nd June 1885

Volume 5

Page	No.	Recipient – Subject matter – Dates
		1302 – 1884-5
436	983	[From Ahmad Suleimān] Flow of goods to Beit al-Māl, sold to raise cash for distribution to Ansār [During 1302] - 22nd Oct 1884-22nd June 1885
437	984	Muhammad al-Nūr Ahmad Permission to read al-Juzūliya collection of supplications [During 1302] - 22nd Oct 1884-22nd June 1885
438	985	[No recipient identified] Description of kiyām prayer, as performed by the Mahdi in Ramadan 1301 [During 1302] - 22nd Oct 1884-22nd June 1885
441	986	[No recipient identified] Description of kiyām prayer, as performed by the Mahdi in Ramadan 1302 [During 1302] - 22nd Oct 1884-22nd June 1885
443	987	[No recipient identified] Quotation and extracts on salāt [During 1302] - 22nd Oct 1884-22nd June 1885
448	988	[No recipient identified] Description of prophetic hadhra, including angel with green crown [During 1302] - 22nd Oct 1884-22nd June 1885
449	989	[No recipient identified] Prophetic hadhra dealing with various matters [During 1302] - 22nd Oct 1884-22nd June 1885

Volume 5

Page	No.	Recipient – Subject matter – Dates
		1302 – 1884-5
452	990	[No recipient identified] Interpretation of the Qurʾān's Sūrat al-Falaq [During 1302] - 22nd Oct 1884-22nd June 1885
454	991	[No recipient identified] Interpretation of the Qurʾān's Sūrat al-Ikhlās [During 1302] - 22nd Oct 1884-22nd June 1885
455	992	[No recipient identified] Details of 7 hadhrāt [on key points of Mahdīa ideology and society] [During 1302] - 22nd Oct 1884-22nd June 1885
457	993	[No recipient identified] Details of 10 hadhrāt [on key points of Mahdīa ideology and society] [During 1302] - 22nd Oct 1884-22nd June 1885
461	994	[No recipient identified] Comment on the baseness of this world [During 1302] - 22nd Oct 1884-22nd June 1885
462	995	[No recipient identified] Description and measurement of Ansār uniform [During 1302] - 22nd Oct 1884-22nd June 1885
463	996	al-Qurāshi Aḥmad al-Kinān Sayings incorporating wise advice [During 1302] - 22nd Oct 1884-22nd June 1885
464	997	[No recipient identified] Womenfolk of Ansār to be called Ansāriyāt, blessing afforded by woman's acceptance of God's path [During 1302] - 22nd Oct 1884-22nd June 1885

Volume 5

Page	No.	Recipient – Subject matter – Dates

1302 – 1884-5

| 465 | 998 | [No recipient identified]
Quotation from the Prophet as heard by Ibrāhīm ibn ʿAlim while working on Sheikh al-Qurāshi's tomb
[During 1302] - 22nd Oct 1884-22nd June 1885 |

Volume 6

Vol 6		Rātib, supplications and sermons
Page	No.	Subject
1	-	Introduction to Rātib and supplications by Dr Muhammad Ibrāhīm Abū-Salīm
36	999	The Rātib
70	1000	Item for inclusion: vision of Makīn Adam al-Humari
71	1001	Supplication from the Rātib
75	1002	Supplication from the Rātib
83	1003	Supplication from the Rātib
85	1004	Supplication from the Rātib
86	1005	Supplications related to postulation
	1006	Supplication from the Rātib
	1007	A humble prayer [ibtihāl]
87	1008	A humble prayer
	1009	A humble prayer
	1010	A supplication
88	1011	A war supplication
	1012	A supplication
	1013	A supplication
	1014	A supplication

Volume 6

Page	No.	Subject
89	1015	A supplication
	1016	Supplication for ritual ablution
91	1017	Supplication of "our father" Adam
	1018	A supplication
91	1019	A supplication
92	1020	A humble prayer
	1021	A supplication
93	1022	A supplication
94	1023	A supplication
	1024	A humble prayer
95	-	Introduction to Sermons [khutub] by Dr Muhammad Ibrāhīm Abū-Salīm
104	1025	All matters in God's hands, call for certainty of belief in God's unity and omnipotence 16th Shawwāl 1301 - 9th August 1884
110	1026	Call for good manners and morals 27th Shaʿbān 1302 - 12th June 1885
119	1027	Sanctity and importance of Ramadan, God's rewards for fasting and overnight prayer
121	1028	Call for jihād and exertion for God like the chosen ones of the past

Volume 6

Page	No.	Subject
126	1029	Work for the eternal after-life rather than this life, doomed to extinction
129	1030	Refrain from deeds that obstruct God's path, regret for those who disobey God
133	1031	Avoid objections to jihād, spend money and exert yourselves for the sake of God
136	1032	Call for jihād
139	1033	Obedience of God at risk of losing this world and the next
142	1034	Cites Hadīth that paradise surrounded by loathsome things, hell the opposite
146	1035	God gives life and takes it away, also guides, instructs feeds and protects
151	1036	Call for obedience, cordiality and purity in serving God
156	1037	Good comes from God alone, rely on him in everything
160	1038	Life is but a dream and illusion, do good deeds, do not waste in lust and pleasure
162	1039	Urges good manners like the Prophet, bad manners poisonous and fatal
167	1040	Call to obey Sunna following call of the Prophet, condemns unlawful things
170	1041	No objections to jihād, give money and life to God and his Prophet

Volume 6

Page	No.	Subject
176	1042	Call for belief in God's unity, uniqueness and omnipotence
186	1043	Anticipation of happy after-life for believers
191	1044	Feed on God's eternal things, not perishable world like animals
195	1045	Praise God who elevates the wretched not the rich or powerful
200	1046	Heed the sūrāt of the Qur'ān and act accordingly
204	1047	Remember the blessings of God the creator of mankind
212	1048	Warning against opposition to God by aspiring to luxuries of the rich
216	1049	Advises those with intelligence not to let their hearts be bewitched
220	1050	Call for reliance on God and submission to his will
226	1051	Reasonable people avoid harm and evil
233	1052	Enumerates blessings of God, advises people not be blind to them
239	1053	Learn from signs and miracles, seek proximity to God
245	1054	Imminent Day of Judgement, warning not to be ashamed before God

Volume 6

Page	No.	Subject
247	1055	World a rotten corpse not worth the wing of a mosquito
251	1056	Support jihād with lives and money, avoiding the fight does not postpone death
253	1057	Importance of learning from history, especially life of Ibrāhīm al-Khalīl
259	1058	Struggle against the self, warning against lustful pleasures
262	1059	Glorious first day of the ʿEid al-Fitr
263	1060	Lists virtues of the ʿEid al-Fitr
265	1061	Call to pay the zakāt of ʿEid al-Fitr
268	1062	Pray to God to bless companions who built basis of Islam [2nd ʿEid al-Fitr sermon]
269	1063	Virtues of sacrifice, guidelines for proper sacrifice
270	1064	[Variation on Sermon 1063]
274	1065	Treat parents well, fear God in dealing with women, pay zakāt

Volume 7

Vol 7		5 collections of majālis ("sessions")
Page	No.	Subject
1	-	Introduction to the majālis by Dr Muhammad Ibrāhīm Abū-Salīm
15	1	Collection of al-Tāhir Muhammad Tātāi [First majlis recorded, on request of Khalīfa 'Abdullāhi]
17	(a)	Sermon: The importance of the Mahdi's sayings
	(b)	Chapter 1: Interpretation of selected verses from the Qur'ān [given in footnotes]
73	(c)	Chapter 2: Sayings of the Mahdi; incidents from the life of the Prophet and various sufis, extolling virtues of jihād; also sayings attributed to the Khalīfa 'Abdullāhi and Khalīfa 'Ali wad Helu [but not Khalīfa Sharīf]
87	(d)	Chapter 3: Sermons and words of wisdom comparing this world with after-life, importance of supplications
109	(e)	Chapter 4: Sermons, proverbs and poetry cited by the Mahdi
113	(f)	Chapter 5: Incantations used by the Mahdi or urged by him to be used
116	(g)	Chapter 6: Quotations and references on the issue of Mahdism and the Mahdi's deeds
127	(h)	Chapter 7: Various issues, including prayers performed by the Mahdi

Volume 7

Page	No.	Subject
141	2	Collection of wad al-Badawi: 9 pages on miscellaneous themes: Purification of hearts through knowledge; instructions on prayers and waterless ablutions; rationale of the dhikr; ethics of the mosque; benefits of attending Mahdi's majālis; inner knowledge [Sufi concept]
187	3	Collection [compiler/scribe unknown]: 87 pages, not sub-divided: Quotations of the Mahdi on jihād and mujāhidīn; extracts from majālis on the lower world and the after-life; quotations from the Prophet, ʿAli ibn Abū-Tālib, Ahmad ibn Hanbal, etc.; verses from the Qurʾān to support arguments
209	4	Collection [compiler/scribe unknown]: 12 pages on miscellaneous themes
211	(a)	Chapter 1: Importance of learning from the Mahdi; instructions on ablution, prayers, incantations and supplications
223	(b)	Chapter 2: Lists loathsome practices [envy, malicious gossip, arrogance, lying, fornication, disloyalty to parents, theft, alcohol, snuff, evading zakāt, impurity]
225	(c)	Chapter 3: Details on prayers; how to call the Adhān; ethics of being in a mosque; how to revere the Mahdi
228	(d)	Chapter 4: Cordiality among Ansār regardless of tribe; fraternity of Ansār above blood relationships; protection of property; virtues of the Mahdi's early companions; virtue of the jibba; war incantation

Volume 7

Page	No.	Subject
237	5	Collection [compiler/scribe unknown]: 47 pages on miscellaneous themes
239	(a)	Chapter 1: Words of wisdom, sayings and sermons comparing this life and the next; value of poverty
	(b)	Chapter 2: Quotations from poetry; also pre-Mahdīa proverbs and sermons
	(c)	Chapter 3: Interpretation of selected verses from the Qurʾān
	(d)	Chapter 4: Funeral prayers; Islamic dress; the turban; breast-feeding as a kinship bond
239	(e)	Chapter 5: Incantations and supplications; wise sayings attributed to the Fourth Khalīfa, etc.
257	-	Maps and photographs of the Mahdīa

Index

Index to Names and Places

Abābda, III/393, 400, V/777, 779, 794
'Abbās (steamer), IV/455, 461
'Abd-al-Bāqi Habīballah, V/926, 927
'Abd-al-Fatāh 'Abdallah, I/11
'Abd-al-Halīm Musā'id, III/424, IV/512, 523, V/804
'Abd-al-Jabbār ibn al-Sheikh Nūr al-Dā'im, II/226, 229
'Abd-al-Karīm Kināni, III/330
'Abdallah Abbūd, III/428, 429
'Abdallah ibn Abū-Bakr, III/320, IV/511, V/750, 755
'Abdallah Ahmad Abū-Sinn, III/394, IV/475, 498, 520, 569, 604, 713
'Abdallah 'Awad al-Karīm Abū-Sinn, IV/458, V/842
'Abdallah al-Mubārak, V/915
'Abdallah ibn Muhammad, IV/553
'Abdallah Muhammad Jubāra, III/434, 450, IV/494
'Abdallah al-Muslimāni, see Lupton, Frank
'Abdallah al-Nūr, I/122, II/190, 191, 196, III/427, IV/469, 470, 481, 486
'Abdallah al-Sanūssi, I/77, 85, 159
'Abdallah al-Tayyib Qamr al-Dīn al-Majdhūb, IV/574, 575
'Abdallah al-Trīfi, V/749
'Abd-al-Mājid Hamad Muhammad Khojali, V/840
'Abd-al-Nabi, I/6
'Abd-al-Qādir Ahmad, IV/609

Index

'Abd-al-Qādir al-Tarīfi, IV/711, 713
'Abd-al-Rahmān Mansūr, I/133
'Abd-al-Rahmān al-Nujūmi, I/77, III/346, 356, 357, 427, IV/458, 464,
    486, 516, 517, 606, 648, 649, 671, 672, 697, 698, 710, 725, 726,
    V/781, 784, 793, 796, 797, 799, 803, 830, 855, 962
'Abd-al-Rahmān al-Qorashi, II/251, IV/460, 505, V/766
'Abd-al-Rahmān Ziyād, V/795
'Abd-al-Samad Sharfi, II/175, 216, 217, 239, III/322, 399, 406, 415,
    422, 423, IV/463
'Abdullāhi Abū-Sinn, V/982
'Abdullāhi al-Khalīfa, I/117, III/448
'Abdullāhi al-Muslimāni, V/932
'Abdullāhi wad al-Nūr, I/104
'Abdullāhi al-Tayyib al-Majdhūb, V/806
Abū-Bakr Ja'far al-Mīrghani, II/187
Abū-Bakr al-Jārkūk, IV/646
Abū-al-Keilik, I/33
Abū-Khumsmā'a, III/310
Abū-Rakham, V/982
Abū-Rof, II/235
"Abū-Rūhein" firearms, V/813
Abū-Sinn clan, III/355, IV/665
Abū-Tulayh, IV/648
Abyssinia, IV/664, 713, V/858
'Adam 'Ali Abū-Jakka, I/27, 28
al-Aghbash ibn al-Basīr, V/950
al-Aghībish, I/28
Ahmad 'Abdallah, V/951
Ahmad 'Abdallah Muhammad Nūr Garāfi, V/830
Ahmad Abū-'Ali, V/742
Ahmad Abū-al-Qāsim, IV/721
Ahmad Abū-Shūq, IV/629
Ahmad al-Aghbash, V/903
Ahmad 'Ali, III/340, 341, 402, V/763
Ahmad ibn al-Amīn, III/435
Ahmad Baqādi, I/65
Ahmad al-Buseiri, IV/713
Ahmad ibn al-Hājj Abū-al-Majdhūb, IV/552
Ahmad al-Hājj al-Badri, I/26, 41, 44, 64, 84, 118

Index

Ahmad ibn al-Hājj Muhammad Zein al-'Abdīn, I/66
Ahmad Hamdān al-'Araki, V/940
Ahmad Hamza, III/336, V/730
Ahmad Hāshim, IV/526, 722
Ahmad 'Iffat, V/748
Ahmad Jafūn, I/172, II/192
Ahmad Jamāl al-Dīn, III/411, 412, 413, IV/557
Ahmad al-Makāshfi, I/136, III/358, IV/549, 657, 658
Ahmad Manūfal, I/77, 78
Ahmad Muhammad 'Abdallah Khojali, IV/719, V/760
Ahmad Muhammad Abū-Sharī'a, IV/495
Ahmad Muhammad al-Fādni, V/907
Ahmad Muhammad al-Hājj Ahmad, II/272
Ahmad ibn Muhammad al-Hājj Sharīf, I/7, IV/583
Ahmad Muhammad al-Jārkūk, IV/645
Ahmad Muhammad Kheir, IV/531, V/795, 799
Ahmad Mustafa, IV/531
Ahmad al-Nūr, III/331, 343, 344, 451, 452, IV/558, 559, 570, 694
Ahmad 'Omar, III/332
Ahmad Pasha, IV/500
Ahmad al-Rayah Dashīn, V/864
Ahmad Sa'ad, III/308
Ahmad Suleimān, I/83, 97, 152, II/188, 189, 202, 203, III/331, 348,
    367, 368, 411, IV/456, 457, 492, 493, 496, 497, 532, 580, 587,
    588, 600, 601, 614, 615, 616, 618, 619, 620, 625, 626, 628, 631,
    633, 634, 635, 636, 637, 638, 642, 646, 663, 686, 721, V/734,
    736, 752, 818, 819, 822, 823, 824, 825, 826, 827, 828, 836, 847,
    851, 874, 875, 876, 877, 878, 886, 888, 890, 900, 915, 916, 917,
    918, 919, 953, 974, 976, 977, 983
Ahmad al-Tayyib al-Basīr, IV/459, 464, 474
Ahmad Yāqūb, III/322
al-'Ajab 'Ali Taha Abū-Jinn, IV/716
'Ajiba bint Bābikr, V/735
'Ali ibn al-Amīn al-Darīr, I/135
'Ali Bakhīt, IV/695
'Ali Hamad Barakāt, IV/607
'Ali Marhūm, IV/534
'Ali Muhammad al-Amīn al-Hindi, V/947
'Ali Muhammad al-Shinturābi, II/275

Index

'Ali Munīr, IV/714
'Ali Mustafa, V/791
'Ali Saʿad Faraj, IV/649, 674, 694, V/751, 800, 896
al-Amīn al-Darīr, I/42, II/245
al-Amīn Muhammad 'Ali Digna, III/379
Amīna Ahmad 'Omar Baqādi, IV/701
Amīna Muhammad Suleimān, V/948
Amir ibn al-Sheikh 'Omar al-Makāshfi, V/951
'Asākir Abū-Kalām, I/29, 34, 35, 36, 40, 47, 63, 84, II/192, IV/692
al-ʿAshābāb, V/777, 798
Ashrāf, I/124, 166, IV/636, V/895
Asta Bilāl, IV/582
Aswan, IV/673
al-ʿAtāya, I/40, 47
Atbara, II/241, III/416
Atbara River, III/316, IV/561, 569, 578
al-ʿAttā al-Manān al-Suleihābi, I/24, 33, 102, 103, 163, 164, III/449, V/775
al-ʿAtta Muhammad al-Dawūd, IV/530
'Awad al-Karīm Ahmad Abū-Sinn, II/222, 223
'Awad al-Karīm al-Kāfūt, IV/510, 595, 681, V/745, 810
Awlād Jubrah clan, V/967
al-ʿAwnīa, IV/485

Bābikr 'Amr, IV/590
Bābikr walad al-Raīs 'Omar, IV/641, 643
Bahr al-Ghazāl, III/417
Bāra, I/77, 121, 131, V/811, 964
Bari, IV/516
Barqu, II/285, 286
al-Bashīr 'Ajab al-Faqīh, V/967
al-Bashīr Muhammad, II/241
al-Bashīr Daw al-Beit, I/36
Bashīr Mustafa Jibrān, V/777, 798
al-Bashīr Nūr al-Dāʿim, I/72, IV/499
al-Bashīr Taha, IV/680
al-Basīr clan, V/903, 904
Batāhīn, II/222
Batta family, I/5

Index

Batūl bint al-Muqaddam, V/887
Beja, IV/632
Beni Amir, V/815
Beni Hamīd, I/74
Beni Hussein, II/200
Berber, II/248, III/312, IV/454, 478, 481, 485, 690, 696, 717, V/731, 771, 794, 872
Bilāl Ramadhān, IV/581, V/802
al-Birka, I/48, II/190
Birashāriyīn, I/109
al-Birka, II/176
Blue Nile, I/33, III/405, IV/548, 651
al-Buqʻa, IV/594
Butrus Salīb, V/761

Copts, V/761, 773

Dafaʻallah Biqwi, I/22
Dāgūri, IV/691
Dāra, II/175, 217, 282, III/322
Darfur, I/38, 95, II/183, 184, 252, 285, 286, IV/508
Daūd Muhammad, V/842
Dār Muhārib, I/59
Dār Umūma, III/398
Daūd Binjah, IV/463
al-Daw wad al-Tayyib, III/429
al-Daw ibn Suleimān (Qādi of Fashoda), I/6
Deim al-Sharq, IV/530
Dongola, III/324, 410, 422, IV/472, 501, 546, 672, 673, 674, 677, 678, 696, 698, 707, 710, V/727, 728, 730, 762, 774, 781, 789, 797, 800, 805, 814, 818, 830, 839, 847, 848
Dūka, II/298
al-Dueim, I/13
Duweih, I/170

Egypt, III/439, IV/673, 708, V/727, 740, 761, 779, 794, 861, 862, 863, 932
Equatoria, IV/468
Eritrea, III/392

160

Index

Fadhalu Ahmad, V/726, 728
Fadl al-Karīm al-Sharīf, IV/521
Fadlallah Ahmad Idrīs, IV/630
Fakhr al-Dīn Hassan al-Maʿalāwi, III/381, 382
Fallāta (West Africans), I/23, 68, III/391, 450, IV/536
al-Faqi Hamīd, III/437
al-Faqi ʿIssa, I/74
al-Faqi Muhammad al-Amīn, III/437
Farajallah Rāghib, IV/473
Farajallah al-Zeini, IV/540
Faraj Azāz, V/746
al-Fasher, I/66, 68, II/218
Fashoda, I/75
Fātima bint Hārūn, IV/562
Fez, V/723, 732, 740, 782
al-Fiteihāb, IV/463
Funj Mountains, I/24

Galābāt, IV/711
Gedaref, IV/475, 489
Gheirhum, I/30
al-Ghobosh, I/88
Gordon Pasha, Colonel Charles, II/261, 262, 263, 264, 265, 266,
    III/397, IV/455, 462, 465, 472, 518, 545, 550, 576, V/854

Habbanīa, III/383
al-Habsha, V/858
Hadendawa, I/109, III/316, 317, V/815
al-Hāj ʿAbdallah, V/908
al-Hāj ʿAbd-al-Qādir, 1/173
al-Hāj ʿAli Muhammad Sālim, V/873
al-Hāj Marzūq, I/60, 82, 127
al-Hāj Sarfi Muhammad, V/772, 773
al-Hāj Sharīf, V/789
al-Hāj al-Sheikh Mahmūd, III/337
al-Hāj al-Tayyib, III/355
al-Hāja Amna, I/8
al-Hāja Zeina, II/179

Index

Halanqa, V/815
Halāwiyīn, I/169, II/251, IV/459, 464, 474, 561
Hamad al-Nīl Hāmid, II/174, 283, III/430, IV/491, 540, 653, V/947
Hamdān Abū-Anja, III/346, 356, 357, IV/660, 662, 668, 669, 670, 685, 692, 693, 700, 706, V/743, 808, 813, 816
Hamdān ibn al-Mak Bashīr, V/790
al-Hankāb, IV/485
al-Haran al-Bashīr, III/400
Harāyna, I/78, 85, 171
Hāshim ibn al-Zubeir, V/928
Hassan ʿAbd-al-Karīm, II/268
Hassan Abū-Sīdein, V/798
al-Hassan Ahmad al-Badawi Hāshi, IV/632, V/865, 866
al-Hassan Ahmad ʿOmar Baqādi, IV/701
al-Hassan Hāshi, V/815
al-Hassan Ibrāhīm Zahrā, V/747, 748, 750, 768
al-Hassan ibn Muhammad ibn ʿAbd-al-Rahmān, V/740
al-Hassan ʿOsmān, IV/698, V/728
al-Hassan Saʿad al-ʿAbādi, V/872
Hassīb, II/219, 220
Hawāzama clan, V/744
Hayāt al-Dīn, IV/534
Hayāt ibn Saʿīd, I/69, 70, 125, II/234, V/852, 867
Hicks Pasha, General William, I/118, 145, 172, II/175, 210, IV/472
al-Hikimdārīa, I/21
Hiyādīa, I/171
Humrān, IV/506, 507
al-Hussein ʿAbd-al-Wāhid, II/241, III/375, 394, IV/513, 514, 547
al-Hussein ʿAli, III/392
Hussein Khalīfa, IV/580, V/727, 742, 777, 779, 780, 794, 798
Hussein [Ibrāhīm] Zahrā, V/770, 840

Ibn ʿArīf Sālih, V/960
Ibrāhīm Adlan, IV/683
Ibrāhīm Ahmad Zerrūq, I/170
Ibrāhīm ibn ʿAlim, V/998
Ibrāhīm Abū-ʿAmūri, IV/563, 565
Ibrāhīm al-Badawi, III/353
Ibrāhīm Dāwi, I/88

Index

Ibrāhīm Hamdūk, IV/624
Ibrāhīm al-Kāshif, V/860
Ibrāhīm Mahmūd, I/10
Ibrāhīm Muhammad al-Dalīl, V/979, 980, 981
Ibrāhīm Muhammad Dhaw, I/113
Ibrāhīm Mustafa, III/350
Ibrāhīm al-Sanūsi al-Hassan, V/733
Idrīs Abū-Ghālib, V/758
Idrīs Ahmad Hāshmi, III/305, 306, 307
Idrīs 'Awād, V/741
Idrīs Muhammad Dawalīb, IV/660, 661
Idrīs al-Sāyir, III/433, V/901
Idrīs Suleimān, IV/703, 704
al-'Ileiqāt, V/742
Ismā'īl Daūd, IV/625, V/822, 824, 826
Ismā'īl Ahmad, V/885, 886
Ismā'īl ibn Ahmad Shadar al-Kheiri, IV/645, 647
'Issa Bedran, V/959

Ja'āfra clan, V/929
Ja'āliyīn, I/110, IV/489, V/731, 815
Jaheina, IV/651
al-Jallāl Muhammad Sharīf, II/280
Jawām'a clan, I/93, 162, V/743
Jazīra, I/46, 169, II/255, III/323, IV/499
Jazīra Aba, I/13
Jebel al-Dāyir, III/318, 346, IV669
Jebel Fungur, I/75
Jebel Gadīr, I/26, 41, 45, 68, IV/669
Jebel al-Harāza, II/230, 295, IV/660
Jebel al-Kadarū, I/49
Jebel Kafāt, V/791
Jebel al-Kanak, V/925
Jebel Massa, III/334
Jebel Najīli, V/790
Jebel Qabā, V/791
Jebel Sodari, V/790
Jebel Tagali, I/23, II/192, III/309, IV/662, 669
Jīballah Mūsa, III/353, 354

Index

Jibr al-Dār al-Hamīdi, I/35
al-Jībrīa, V/829, 831
Jihādīa, II/253, IV/606
al-Jīra, IV/713
Johannes, V/858
Judge Mirghani, III/330
al-Juheina clan, I/32
al-Jumaʿ clan, IV/706
al-Juzūliya supplications, V/984

Kababish, I/32
Kalogi Hills, I/27, 28
Kāmlīn, IV/500
Karamallah Sheikh Muhammad, III/351, 352, 388, 389
Karari, IV/618
Kassala, V/740, 747, 748, 750, 753, 755, 757, 765

Khalīfa ʿAbdullāhi, I/73, 81, 100, 121, 128, 132, 144, 162, 166, 167,
    II/215, 242, 259, 296, 297, 298, III/330, 332, 349, 360, 385,
    396, 425, 436, 438, 446, 447, IV/484, 516, 529, 543, 549, 573,
    577, 584, 591, 592, 606, 621, 627, 644, 647, 665, 679, 688, 695,
    700, V/848, 849, 850, 851, 871, 894, 920, 921, 922, 923, 933,
    955, 959, 960, 961, 962, 963, 964, 965, 966, 967, VII/1
Khalīfa ʿAli wad al-Helu, II/276, 277, IV/592, V/967
Khalīfa Dirdīri, IV/661
Khalīfa Muhammad Sharīf, III/384, IV/582, 606, 627, V/803, 811, 955
al-Khalīfa al-Sheikh ʿAttā al-Manān, I/25
al-Khalīfa al-Sheikh Muhammad, V/911
Khalīl Hussein, II/198
Khandaq, V/814
Khartoum, II/182, 205, 221, 251, 278, 284, 290, 293, III/300, 301, 388,
    405, 406, 413, 416, 421, IV/492, 502, 519, 521, 522, 533, 541,
    544, 550, 551, 563, 565, 577, 578, 584, 585, 588, 589, 590, 596,
    597, 598, 601, 602, 603, 604, 605, 608, 610, 620, 641, 690,
    V/823, 959
Khashm al-Mūs Bak, IV/483
Khatmīa, II/187, III/374
al-Khawāja Georgios Salīb, V/761

Index

Khor al-Tayyir, I/30
Kordofan, I/78, 83, II/261, III/360, 398, 422, IV/679, 695

Lūqāt, I/28
Lupton, Frank, IV/468

Ma'āqila, I/85
Maghreb, IV/724
Mahmūd 'Abd-al-Qādir, I/74, 75, 76, 79, 106, II/284, 295, III/309, 310, 321, 342, 362, 363, 366, 387, 393, 400, 401, 417, 422, 424, 450, IV/462, 508, 533, 546, 566, 594, 597, 669, 670, 679, 693, 705, V/756, 816, 856, 857
Mahmūd al-Hāj Muhammad, III/411, 412, 413
Mahmūd 'Issa Zā'id, III/338, 394, IV/555, 602, 664
Mahmūd walad al-Khabīr, I/119
al-Majdhūb Abū-Bakr Yūsuf, IV/541, V/806
al-Majdhūb Hussein, IV/691
al-Mak 'Adam, II/192, 242, III/334
al-Makāshfi clan, V/955
al-Mak 'Omar 'Adam, I/54, II/258
al-Mak 'Osmān, IV/676
Mali, V/852, 867
al-Malik 'Abd-al-Rahmān, III/303
Manah clan, IV/700
al-Manna Ismā'īl, I/93, 94, 101, 114, 120
al-Mardi Abū-Rof, IV/521
Marrakesh, V/733, 776, 782
al-Massallamīa, IV/548
Mauretania, V/853
Mecca, I/173
Metemma, IV/502, 546, 694, 708, 710, V/800, 803, 896
Mīrghani Muhammad Sālih, IV/698
Mīrghani Suwār al-Dahab, III/426, V/728
Misairīa, III/391
Morocco, V/740, 758
al-Mudatthir Ibrāhīm, III/442, V/786, 787, 891, 892
Muhammad 'Abd-al-Karīm, IV/648, 652, 656, 657, 715, 720, V/764, 788, 832, 833, 841
Muhammad 'Abdallah, I/133

Index

Muhammad 'Abd-al-Qādir, V/772, 773
Muhammad ibn 'Abd-al-Qādir ibn 'Abd-al-Karīm, V/973
Muhammad 'Abd-al-Rahīm, III/332
Muhammad 'Abd-al-Salām, V/733
Muhammad 'Abū-Bakr Ja'far al-Mīrghani, V/753
Muhammad Abū-Hijil, IV/461, 504, 613
Muhammad Ahmad Abū-Shūq, IV/628
Muhammad Ahmad al-Badawi, V/845, 846
Muhammad ibn Ahmad Dafa'allah, I/89
Muhammad Ahmad Hāshim, IV/722
Muhammad Ahmad Jalāl-al-Dīn al-Majdhūb, V/738
Muhammad Ahmad Shaddād, IV/705
Muhammad Ahmad al-Suleihābi, V/775
Muhammad Ahmad Umm Bireir, IV/455
Muhammad 'Ali Kartūb, IV/560, 578
Muhammad 'Ali Qurāfi, II/292
Muhammad 'Ali al-Toam, V/854
Muhammad al-Amīn Ahmad, V/852
Muhammad al-Amīn al-Fulāti, III/335
Muhammad ibn Amir, V/821
Muhammad Arbāb, IV/711, V/859
Muhammad Babikr, IV/654
Muhammad Bābikr al-Suleihābi, IV/712
Muhammad al-Badawi al-Sidcīq, IV/677
Muhammad al-Badawi Abū-Safīya, III/309, IV/571
Muhammad ibn al-Hājj Ahmad, I/90
Muhammad al-Amīn, I/46
Muhammad al-Amīn Ahmad, V/867
Muhammad al-Amīn Dafa'allah, III/384, 385
Muhammad al-Amīn al-Darīr, IV/590
Muhammad al-Badawi Abū-Safīya, I/149
Muhammad Bashīr, IV/639
Muhammad Beni Rāghib, IV/554
Muhammad al-Dādādi, I/43, 56
Muhammad Dawalīb, IV/661
Muhammad al-Dawi al-Sādiq al-Kināni, IV/678
Muhammad al-Faqi Ahmad, III/416
Muhammad al-Faqih Hamad, IV/560, 561
Muhammad Fawzi Mahmūd, V/895

Index

Muhammad al-Hājj Ahmad, I/155, 156
Muhammad al-Ghāli ʿAbd-al-Salām, V/732, 733
Muhammad walad Hamad, III/316
Muhammad Ibrāhīm Dāwi, IV/506, 507, 510
Muhammad Imām, V/868
Muhammad Ismāʿīl, V/951
Muhammad Jibrīl, V/769, 791
Muhammad Karīb, IV/592
Muhammad Khālid Zughul, II/183, 184, 218, 220, 252, 253, 256, 267, III/320, 359, 370, 383, 391, 395, 406, 408, 410, 422, IV/511, 515, 536, 566, 567, 603
Muhammad Khalīl, IV/652, 680
Muhammad al-Kheir ʿAbdallah Khojali, II/240, 248, 275, 288, III/312, 313, 336, 403, 404, IV/454, 461, 477, 478, 480, 503, 525, 527, 535, 613, 649, 655, 671, 673, 698, 703, 710, 718, 719, 722, V/727, 730, 731, 738, 751, 759, 760, 781, 783, 792, 794, 795, 796, 797, 799, 839, 872, 939
Muhammad al-Kheir Baʿdi, IV/566, 567
Muhammad al-Kheir Idrīs, III/370
Muhammad al-Mādih, V/949
Muhammad al-Mahdi al-Sanūssi, I/115, 116, II/285
Muhammad ibn Mahmūd, V/844
Muhammad al-Mak Nāsir, IV/676
Muhammad al-Malīkān, I/127
Muhammad al-Malik Hamad, V/860
Muhammad Musāʿid, III/387
Muhammad al-Mustafa ibn al-Imām, V/937
Muhammad Nabawi, V/870
Muhammad al-Nūr Ahmad, V/984
Muhammad Nūr ibn Hasana, V/928
Muhammad Nūr Mahmūd ʿAbd-al-Rahman, III/411, 412, IV/557
Muhammad ʿOmar al-Banna, III/331
Muhammad ʿOsmān ʿAbdallah, V/837, 838
Muhammad ʿOsmān Abū-Girja, II/146, 255, 259, 281, III/427, IV/458, 464, 572, 573, 598, 599, 600, 648, 649, 671, 672, 697, 726, V/793, 800, 926
Muhammad ʿOsmān Khālid, IV/665, V/807, 832, 833
Muhammad ʿOsmān al-Mīrghani, III/390, V/807
Muhammad ʿOsmān Muhammad Farah, V/802

Index

Muhammad 'Osmān ibn al-Sayyid al-Hassan Al-Mīrghani, II/199
Muhammad ibn Rahmatallah, V/942
Muhammad al-Raqīq, I/48, 129, 130, 154
Muhammad Sa'īd, V/916
Muhammad Sālih Sāti, IV/501, V/834, 835, 839, 860, 974
Muhammad Sālih Suwār al-Dahab, II/178, V/910
Muhammad Sharīf 'Abd-al-Hai, V/982
Muhammad Sharīf Nūr al-Dā'im, I/153, II/260, III/328, V/889
Muhammad al-Sirāj ibn Muhammad al-Nūr, I/126
Muhammad Suleimān, IV/482, 568, 627, 652, 657, 665, 666, 667, V/898, 960
Muhammad Tāhir 'Abdallah, IV/528
Muhammad al-Tāhir ibn al-Tayyib Qamr al-Dīn al-Majdhūb, II/206, III/376, 377
Muhammad Taqi al-Dīn, V/853
Muhammad al-Taweim, I/98, 150, 151, 165, IV/490, 541
Muhammad al-Tayyib al-Basīr, I/12, 15, 169, II/204, 223, 225, 226, 227, 232, 250, 254, 255, 299, III/428, IV/699, V/868, 894, 935, 936
Muhammad al-Tayyib Qamr al-Dīn al-Majdhūb, IV/702
Muhammad al-Tayyib al-Suleihābi, II/235, IV/650, 712
Muhammad Umm Baddah, V/924
Muhammad Yūsuf, II/285, 286
Muhammadein al-'Areiq, I/99
Mulazimīn, I/157, III/407
al-Munshatih Karrār, V/778
Mūsa Ahmad al-Bashīr al-Khanfari, I/59
Mūsa Muhammad al-Ahmar, I/14, 39
al-Musharraf Muhammad, IV/752
Mustafa 'Ali Hadal, III/317, IV/506, 595, 596, 681, V/745, 767, 810
Mustafa Yāwir, III/324, 410, IV/707, V/814

al-Naf'āb clan, IV/703, 704
al-Namā, II/238
Nasīm ibn Adawi, IV/655
Nawāy Deifallah, V/744
Nuba Mountains, I/49, 54, 55, 75, III/321, 378, 450
al-Nūr ibn al-Fuqara al-Jabarti, IV/691
al-Nūr Ibrāhīm, V/884

Index

al-Nūr Muhammad Angara, IV/571, 674, 677
Nusshi Pasha, IV/484
Nuwāi Seifallah, V/816

al-'Obeid, I/48, 50, 51, 52, 74, 80, 104, 123, 131, II/249, III/360, 423, 424, IV/480, V/811
'Omar 'Adam, I/55
'Omar Digna, III/378
'Omar Ilyās, I/99, 146, II/217
'Omar Muhammad Kheir Terhu, IV/567
Omdurman, IV/472, 473, 533, 543, 551, 594, 618, 664, 674, 677, 679, 720, V/756, 783, 810, 823
'Osmān Abū-Girja, I/34
'Osmān Digna, I/110, 111, 112, II/206, 208, 209, 210, 240, 273, 274, III/315, 317, 369, 371, 373, 374, 376, 378, 390, IV/507, 551, 560, 632, V/755, 757, 765, 810, 815, 820, 844, 865, 866
'Osmān Sālih Arbāwi, IV/512
'Oweidha, II/200

Pain, Olivier, III/393, 400
Prophet Muhammad, I/52, 71, III/308, 325, 359, IV/495, 687, V/906, 940, 949, 998, VI/1039, 1040, 1041

Qādi al-Islam, I/107, III/340, 341, 402, V/763
Qaili wad al-Ati, III/355
Qeirā, V/769
Qomā, V/769
al-Qurāshi Ahmad al-Kinān, V/996
al-Qurāshi al-Tayyib al-Basīr, II/228, V/881
al-Qur'ān, II/233, III/347, 419, IV/552, 617, 723, V/940, 952, 990, 991, VI/1046

al-Rahad, II/293
Rahma Manūfal, I/146, IV/679
Rahma Muhammad Sa'īd, V/829, 831

Index

Rātib, II/252, IV/538, 574, 593, 617, V/734, 979, 980, 981, VI/999, 1000, 1001, 1002, 1003, 1004, 1005, 1006
Rawāwiqa, II/236
Rizeigāt, I/130
Rubātab, IV/461
al-Rufāʿa, III/405, 449, IV/458, 651, V/909

Saʿad Ahmad Badr, IV/529
Saʿad Farah, IV/502
Saʿad Sālim, V/751
al-Sabalūqa Gorge, IV/522, 531
al-Sadīq al-Ḥājj Ahmad Hadhra, I/134, II/211
Saʿīd walad Bata, IV/715
Saʿīd Nasr, III/329, 384
Salāmat al-Bāsha, II/282
Sālih walad Fadlallah al-Kabāshi, I/32, II/270
Salih Hussein Khalīfa, IV/503, 535
Sālih al-Mak, II/224, 299, IV/465, 466, 467, V/871
Sālih al-Takrūri, IV/664
Samīm clan, V/920
Sammānīa, I/1
al-Samni Ahmad, IV/513
Sāti Ahmad, I/86
al-Sawārāb, IV/485, 530
al-Sāyir, IV/592
al-Sayyid ʿAbd-al-Rāziq, V/876
al-Sayyid Muhammad ʿOsmān al-Mīrghani, V/770
al-Sayyid Muhammad ibn al-Sayyid Musāʿid, II/240, 288
al-Sayyid Tāha, V/968
Sayyidein Yūnus al-Burdanein, IV/563
Sennār, IV/499, 648, 652, 656, 657, 658, 668, 676, V/762, 788, 801, 841
Shāb Dīnāb, I/109
Shakka, II/282
al-Shāmi Abū-Safīa, I/117
Shāmi Habāni, IV/678
al-Sharīf Ahmad Taha, II/241, III/329
al-Sharīf Hamad al-Nīl, III/438, V/975
al-Sharīf Suleimān al-ʿUbeid, II/188
Shāt, V/899

Index

Shāyib Ahmad, V/728
al-Sheikh ʿAbd-al-Rasūl, I/45
al-Sheikh Ahmad ibn al-Hājj Bābikr, I/67
al-Sheikh Ahmad al-Jaʿali, III/311
al-Sheikh ʿAli walad Tāhir, I/38
al-Sheikh Bābikr Saʿīd, I/67, III/334
al-Sheikh Bireir, I/50
al-Sheikh Fādhlu Ahmad, IV/600, 610
al-Sheikh Idris walad al-Arbāb, IV/607
al-Sheikh Muhammad Sharīf Nūr al-Dāʾim, I/3, II/227, III/396
al-Sheikh Mūsa, IV/591
al-Sheikh al-Nayal, V/927
al-Sheikh al-Qorashi, I/106, V/998
al-Sheikh Suleimān, I/9, 13, 23, 45, 62
al-Sheikh Tāha Bashīr, V/897
al-Sheikh al-Tayyib, II/227
al-Sheikh al-ʿUbeid wad Badr, II/238, 251
Shendi, IV/502
Shilluk, II/201, 237
Shingetti, III/374
Shinqīt, V/853
Shukrīa clan, III/316, IV/560, 578, 595
Shurkeila, II/293
Sirāj al-Dīn, I/1
al-Sirāj al-Hājj al-Daw, II/269
Siyāq, II/201
Slatin, Rudolf, II/282, V/899, 900
Suakin, I/104, 111, 112, II/208, III/369, 371
Sufi, III/437
Suleimān Garjāj, V/751
Suleimān Sālih, II/293
Suleimān al-ʿUbeid, V/947
Sunna, I/58, IV/723, VI/1040
Sureihāt, I/171
al-Surra bint al-Naʿma, III/372

Taha ʿAbd-al-Bāqi, V/914
Taha al-Bashīr, I/58
Taha Muhammad, V/878

Index

al-Tāhir al-Majdhūb, IV/617
al-Tāhir Muhammad Tātāi, IV/513, 605, 711, 713, V/749, VII/1
al-Tāhir al-Tījāni, II/267, III/399, 408
Taka, I/109, V/746, 754
Tamām tribe, I/55
al-Tayyib Ahmad Hāshim, IV/524, V/776
al-Tayyib al-Banāni, IV/717, V/758, 759, 782
al-Tayyib ibn Muhammad al-Tayyib al-Majdhūb, I/110
al-Tayyib Nūr al-Dā'im, IV/500
al-Tayyib Suleihābi, V/788
al-Tayyiba, IV/505
Tureifia, I/171, II/272

al-'Ubeid Badr, II/204, 205, 221, IV/579, 580
al-'Ubeid Muhammad Sa'īd, V/827, 829
Usman Dan Fodio, I/125

Wad Medani, IV/474, V/864
al-Wāliya clan, V/926, 927
West Africa, V/776
White Nile, I/119
Wolseley, General Lord Garnet, V/774

Yūsuf Hassan al-Shallāli, I/31. 60
Yūsuf al-Hindi, I/46
Yūsuf Suleimān, IV/639

Zaghāwa, I/95, II/219
Zarūq al-Tāhir, IV/564
al-Zubeir al-Fahl, I/86
al-Zubeir Rahma, IV/709, V/855

Index to Topics

bayʿa, III/351, V/782, 806
Beit al-Māl, I/97, 139, 159, II/202, 244, III/335, 348, 367, 434, 441,
    IV/454, 476, 478, 492, 519, 582, 583, 592, 625, 628, 630, 684,
    689, 699, V/736, 749, 783, 809, 820, 836, 849, 851, 869, 885,
    900, 973, 983
"Daʿwa Proclamation", I/21, 37, 86, 116
divorce, II/250, III/364, 365, IV/457, 542, V/741, 897
dowry, I/76, 165, III/365, IV/610, V/971
hadhra, I/11, 15, 16, 21, 71, 110, II/232
ʿEid al-Fitr, VI/1059, 1060, 1061, 1062
hijra, I/15, 17, 18, 20, 29, 34, 37, 39, 43, 44, 69, 133, 134, 139, 153,
    II/211, 221, 292, III/413, 418, 443, IV/527, V/937, 950
jihād, I/21, 24, 54, 75, 91, 115, 124, 138, 139, 171, II/184, 208, 211, 240,
    241, 248, 249, 253, III/311, 409, 414, 418, 431, 443, IV/470,
    495, 504, 552, 606, 612, 723, V/868, 969, VI/1028, 1031, 1032,
    1041, 1056, VII/1(c), 3
land, III/345, 353, 354, 403, 404, IV/477, 400, 675, V/821
legal issues, I/58, 168, II/212, 213, 239, 277, III/351, 354, IV/548,
    V/736, 812, 838, VI/1040 (see also: Sharīʿa)
marriage, I/4, III/305, 306, 307, 403, IV/456, 457, 562, 598, 599, 608,
    716, V/881, 891, 892, 896, 897, 903, 959, 973, 977
polygamy, IV/542

Index

property, I/35, 76, 83, II/258, 260, 270, 276, III/330, 351, 352, 354, 373, 391, 395, 408, IV/477, 512, 522, 543, 577, 589, 591, 595, 630, 689, 700, V/752, 821, 923, 948, 961, VII/4(d)

Sharī'a, I/ 58, II/176, 195, 271, III/341, 358, IV/548

slavery, I/2, 61, 79, II/230, III/366, 367, IV/620, 621, 628, 666, 667, 717, V/731, 812, 876, 877, 916, 953, 959

tax, III/403 (see also: zakāt)

'ulamā', I/52, 160, V/862, 909

zakāt, III/383, IV/671, 680, V/749, 838, 930, 1065

www.ingramcontent.com/pod-product-compliance
Lightning Source LLC
Chambersburg PA
CBHW061647040426
42446CB00010B/1627